Trains on th

The Railways of Llanymynech

& Pant

Neil Rhodes

COVER PHOTO *Looking down on Pant Station on September 9, 1964, the railway winding away towards Llanymynech (Joan Jones)*
TITLE PAGE *Llanymynech station at its finest: Churchward Mogul 4300 Class 2-6-0 6371 from Welshpool arrives to pick up passengers for Oswestry*
BACK COVER PHOTO *7800 Torquay Manor arrives at Llanymynech with the 08.20 Oswestry to Aberystwyth train on September 2, 1961 (Gerald T Robinson)*

To John Humphreys
Without whose help, encouragement, enthusiasm, and especially information, I could not have produced this book

NR

Published by Neil Rhodes Books
Well Cottage
Wern
Llanymynech
SY22 6PF
nr@neilrhodes.co.uk

www.neilrhodesbooks.com

British Library Cataloguing in Publication Data
A catalogue record for this book is available from the British Library

ISBN 978-0-9555557-3-2

Printed by Counter Print
Stafford
ST16 3AX
01785 241404
www.counterprint.co.uk

Contents

What might have happened – but didn't   5

Early transport in Llanymynech   7

Early railway plans   8

The Oswestry & Newtown Railway   9

The opening of the Oswestry & Newtown Railway   19

The Llanfyllin railway   21

The Cambrian Railways   24

The West Shropshire Mineral Railway   28

The Potteries, Shrewsbury and North Wales Railway   32

The judge and the railway guard   38

The Nantmawr branch   40

The Wern junction accident   43

Llanymynech signal box   45

The Pant heiress and the railway porter   47

The Shropshire & Montgomeryshire Railway   53

The Great Western Railway   65

Carreghofa Halt   73

Llanymynech Station   76

The S&MLR & the War Department   87

The Humphreys railway family   89

Four Crosses Station   90

Pant Station   94

Llanymynech & British Railways   98

The death of Llewelyn Jones   102

The Llanfyllin line   106

The closure of the Shropshire & Montgomeryshire   119

The threat of closure   131

Closure & demolition   136

Last thoughts   140

Acknowledgements

This book concerns the railways of Llanymynech and Pant, though I've widened the area slightly to include Four Crosses, as well as any part that affected Llany- mynech, like the Llanfyllin branch. I intended it to be comprehensive, but as with all things the more you delve the more you realize how much you don't know. I would like to thank the many people who have helped in the writing of this book, and the collecting of the various photographs. John and Sheila Humphreys have been especially helpful, as have Mike Robinson, Brian Rowe, Roger Date, RS Carpenter, RC Casserley, Willy Cossey, Colin Jenkins, Joan Jones, Russell Mulford, Neil Parkhouse, Gerald T Robinson, and all other photographers or collectors. Also I would like to thank Su Perry at the Oswestry Advertizer for allowing me to use some of the Advertizer material, and Derek Williams and the staff at Oswestry library, who have as always been extremely helpful in letting me look at their stock of local history material, as have the Oswestry Council at the Guildhall. I would also like to thank my wife, Pauline Rhodes, for her proofread- ing and suggestions, though I accept responsibility for all mistakes. I've tried very hard to contact all photographers or collections, but apologise if I've been unsuccessful, or have inadvertently credited the wrong person. I've changed the images digitally only to repair scratches and so on, or to enhance fading contrast or colour.

Llanymynech before the railways: a field map, showing the canal and tramways (in the two Railway Fields at top left). The railways of the future are shown faintly. The station took the Field below the Village and most of Cae Newydd

The Crewe of the Welsh borders

WHAT MIGHT HAVE HAPPENED — BUT DIDN'T

Llanymynech was a small and insignificant village until 1860. Then the Oswestry and Newtown Railway, going through Llanymynech from the north to the south, was opened, and in 1866 the Shrewsbury and North Wales Railway was built from the east to the west. Both railways were part of larger schemes which might have stayed as mere dreams, if it hadn't been that larger companies put up huge amounts of money.

First, the Shrewsbury and North Wales Railway was seen by the Great Western Railway as a way to get to Ireland and rival the London & North Western Railway's route via Holyhead. After all, the great Isambard Kingdom Brunel had suggested that way to Dublin, which persuaded the GWR to put money forward to drive a railway through the Cambrian Mountains, to Dolgellau and Porthmadog, and across the Llyn peninsula to Porth Dinlleyn, where a port was built, a port that was in quieter waters than Holyhead. So, with a connection at Shrewsbury, a great route was opened from Stoke-on-Trent and Birmingham, and eventually from London, through to Dublin. Old GWR plans to open Fishguard as a port were abandoned, as Porth Dinlleyn was so much nearer than Fishguard to the important city of Dublin.

Second, while this was happening, the great trunk line from Manchester to Milford Haven was being built. Manchester and Liverpool were always great rivals, and because Manchester resented the power Liverpool had over it as a port, it wanted a new harbour for its cotton from America. The Oswestry and Newtown Railway had been built mainly as a single track railway but had

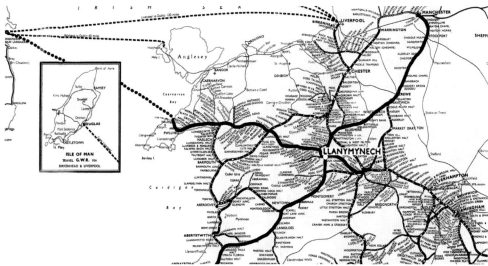

An imaginary idea of how a GWR railway map might have looked, if all the plans had come to anything: with Llanymynech as the great junction of Wales and the Midlands

bridges capable of being strengthened and doubled, and the great main line was soon being built section by section. Of course, as with the Shrewsbury and North Wales Railway, there were problems, but the obstacle of the Cambrian Mountains, between Llangurig and Strata Florida, was overcome with a long tunnel, and so the great route was opened.

The two great trunk lines, the Great Western Railway from London to Dublin, and the Cambrian Railways from Manchester to Milford Haven, crossed at the by now very important junction of Llanymynech. Of course that meant a large and well-proportioned station, and it seemed an obvious place to put the new locomotive works (though other places were suggested, including the now insignificant little market town of Oswestry to the north). Freight and passenger traffic grew, as did the town, which became, like Crewe, a true railway town. When the Great Western Railway took over the Cambrian Railways in 1922, the junction at Llanymynech naturally increased in importance, the station and freight area alone becoming as large as the whole of the original village. There was some talk in the 1960s of both routes being threatened with closure, but luckily common sense prevailed, and the line from Manchester to South Wales and the one from Shrewsbury to North Wales are now considered two of the most important routes through Britain. The position and status of Llanymynech at the junction of these two lines is secure.

Of course it wasn't inevitable that Llanymynech should have become the most important town in the whole of the Welsh Marches. It needed the vision and investment of those Victorian bankers and entrepreneurs, so luck had something to do with it. On the other hand, it's possible to see that Llanymynech is perfectly placed, situated as it is right on the border between England and Wales, yet at the end of a westward valley, the entrance to Mid Wales, and with its own resources of lime and stone.

Such is the size and importance of Llanymynech in the 21st century, there are even calls for the town to be made into a city, the only one in the UK to be in two countries. And there seems to be only one major obstacle to that event taking place: English people still can't pronounce it properly.

Naturally, all that didn't happen. Most people would say it never could have happened, mainly because the Cambrian Mountains are too expensive to cut through for the amount of freight and number of passengers the lines would have taken. But a tunnel of two miles was built on the very minor line from Conway to Blaenau Ffestiniog, a line that ended at a small terminus. It's certainly possible to imagine two similar tunnels, one through the Berwyn Mountains to Bala, and another beyond Llangurig. And in the minds of the railway investors it was not only feasible but expected that there would be two major routes – Manchester to Milford Haven and the Midlands to Dublin – and the place the lines crossed was Llanymynech.

From the Romans to the tramways

EARLY TRANSPORT IN LLANYMYNECH

Llanymynech, since prehistoric times, had been an important transport hub, because it had mineral wealth, especially lead, zinc, and copper, and the minerals needed to be moved. Probably the River Vyrnwy had always been used, down its eight or so winding miles to the Severn. The Romans would have built stronger roads in the area, and though a Roman road has not been definitely identified, it is possible there was one along the now minor road between Crickheath and Morton.

When the limestone from Llanymynech Hill was quarried in significant amounts, the main problem was transport. The Vyrnwy was used, and carts and donkeys along the primitive roads, but this was still very difficult and slow. In 1796 a breakthrough was made when the Ellesmere Canal was built. At last large amounts of limestone could be moved, either up the Severn valley (when the Montgomeryshire Canal to Newtown was finished in 1821) to improve the land, or more importantly eastwards to the Midlands and the north of England for steelmaking and other industries. There was still the problem of bringing the limestone from the hill down to the canal, and this is where Llanymynech had its first railways, in the form of narrow gauge tramways.

It's not known exactly when the tramways were built on Llanymynech Hill, but it wasn't before 1796, when the canal was opened (though tramways did exist before then in other parts of the country). In fact they almost certainly weren't built before 1817, because the one in Welshpool from Stondart Quarries to the Montgomeryshire Canal was built then, famously being the first railway to fit rails into chairs.

The tramways were mostly two foot gauge. On the level or slight gradients they were generally horse-drawn, or used gravity on the incline plane (a truck full of limestone connected to a cable that went round the gin wheel and pulled up an empty truck that was connected to the other end of the cable). In other places the rockmen (the workers in the quarry) simply pushed the trucks.

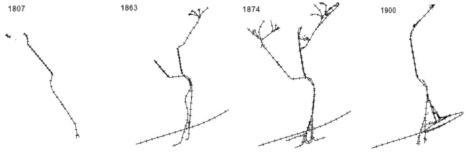

Tramways of Llanymynech going to the canal, at 1807, 1863, 1874 & 1900 (CPAT)

Tracks to everywhere

EARLY RAILWAY PLANS

The middle of the 19th century was an extraordinary time for the planning and building of the new transport system: the railways with their fast and powerful steam locomotives. When the fastest transport had been horses, which could only go a few miles an hour for short distances, and the best transport for bulk the canals, which took several days to go from Llanymynech to Birmingham), it's easy to see the revolution that was the new railways. Having a railway line meant the modern world had reached your area.

Plans were proposed all over the country, and no fewer in Wales and the borders. Brunel and the GWR had a scheme to go across to Wales from Shrewsbury to Barmouth and up to Porth Dinlleyn, but this was abandoned when the London & North Western Railway opened the North Wales coast route to Holyhead. Porth Dinlleyn was not abandoned as an idea for a port to Ireland, and nor was Milford Haven as a port to America, even though it had lost its status as a Royal Dockyard. The Manchester and Milford Railway was proposed to go from Crewe to Llanymynech (avoiding Oswestry!) and on to Newtown, Llanidloes, and through the mountains to Pembrokeshire.

Even before the railway network reached Oswestry (and this was only via a branch line from the main Shrewsbury to Chester line, something that was caused by the intransigence of certain local landowners, a fact that was deeply resented in the area) there was talk of spreading out into Wales and the border country. The Shropshire Union Company had obtained an act for making a line from Newtown to Oswestry in 1846, but they had allowed the powers of their act to expire.

In 1852 there were at least two plans in progress. The first was a line from Shrewsbury to Aberystwyth, with a branch line to Oswestry from Welshpool. The second was a main trunk line from Oswestry to Newtown. Both lines would have gone through Llanymynech, but the second was preferred, because that was a main as opposed to a branch line. The Oswestry & Border Counties Advertiser said, "No person who will take the trouble of opening a map of England and Wales can for a moment question, that the most advantageous communications for all parties will provide that the main trunk line should go through Oswestry, and it is not less due to the interests of the great Northern manufacturing districts, than it is to ourselves, to withhold our sanction from any project which does not involve this as an integral part of its design."

The Montgomeryshire Railway was the name of the second plan, the one that Oswestry wanted, especially as it would include a new railway station, and the Great Western station was considered very unpleasant. Also, as soon as the GWR connected Shrewsbury to Wolverhampton, they put the prices up from 3 to 7 pence a ticket – unsurprisingly, the company was not liked in the area.

The railway reaches Llanymynech

THE OSWESTRY & NEWTOWN RAILWAY

A public meeting was held in Oswestry in November 1854, when it was proposed that a railway should be built from Newtown to Oswestry, as an extension of the Newtown and Llanidloes line that was currently being built. This plan was roughly the same as the Montgomeryshire Railway scheme. The bill for this 'Oswestry, Welshpool, and Newtown Railway' came before the House of Commons on Monday, 7 June, 1855. Six months later money for the Shrewsbury and Welshpool Railway was raised, with the proposal: "The object of the undertaking is to connect the County of Montgomery, the mineral district of the Rea Valley, and the Llanymynech lime rocks, with Shrewsbury, the Midland counties, and London" – though of course that railway never reached Llanymynech.

On 14 January 1857 it was reported that land and valuers were engaged in purchasing the land for the Oswestry and Newtown Railway, and an announcement was made on July 15 in the Advertiser that the first sod of the 'Oswestry, Welshpool, and Newtown Railway' was going to be cut. "The ceremony will take place near the Bowling Green, Welshpool, and it is supposed that Lady Williams Wynn will cut the first sod." Though in the same edition the company was called the Oswestry and Newtown Railway Company, and this continued.

The ceremony to cut the first sod of the Oswestry & Newtown Railway at Welshpool, August 4, 1857, as the guns of Powis Castle boomed

The suggestion that Welshpool should be the place where the ceremony of cutting the first sod took place was resented in Llanymynech. An article, presumably meant to be humorous, said that there was a meeting in Llanymynech to debate the proposal that as there was no castle within 5 miles of Llanymynech, it would be a better place for the ceremony of cutting the first sod than Welshpool, and "that should the people of Welshpool persist in having the ceremony performed in that place, a body of the Llanymynech Rockmen should be sent on the day appointed to stop the proceedings. No man was of a more peaceable disposition than the writer but he felt he had a duty to perform and he for one should do his duty. He had no doubt but that the proprietors of the canal would lend a supply of boats for the conveyance of the Rockmen, for he was well assured that it was far from their wish that the sod should be cut at all. The Prince of Wales had expressed his readiness to visit Llanymynech the purpose of trying on his boots and turning the sod." Llanymynech rockmen were renowned throughout the area for their ability to pick fights and win them.

After the cutting of the first sod ceremony was over, the Advertiser said on August 12, 1857: "Our readers will be gratified to know that the works have actually commenced, and that on Monday last two waggon loads of planks and barrows were conveyed from the Oswestry Railway Station to the Pant, where land has been engaged for the reception of the plant. In a few days we may expect an inundation of Navvies, and confidently hope our prophecy will be fulfilled of seeing a railway to Llanymynech by Christmas!" This optimism was misplaced.

The first contractors were Messrs Thornton & McCormack. There was a report on the progress of the railway works in the Advertiser edition of October 21, which stated that the works were proceeding with considerable spirit and energy. The article provides an interesting description of the methods used in making a railway. The place described is in Pant (which was then called 'the Pant'), between the bottom of Rhew Revel Lane and the bottom of Station Road.

> The cuttings commenced at the Pant, on the left-hand side of the turnpike road leading from Oswestry to Welshpool, – near to, and on the right-hand side of, the canal, going in the same direction.
> When the works were first begun, very few men were employed for some time, as they had to cut through what is called a "rotten rock". Having made commencement of that place, additional hands were put on from time to time, and the fruits of their labours have become somewhat extensive, and are more and more evident every day. There are now in constant employ about 100 men, including (principally) navvies, carpenters, blacksmiths, and masons. There are, also, six horses employed, which are used for drawing the ballast waggons or earth trucks, the removal of large

stones, or pieces of rock, and other such like purposes. Ten or a dozen ballast waggons are in use, but there are at the place nearly thirty others lying idle, which led us to hope that the energetic contractor will speedily commence on a still more extensive scale.

The rotten rock is still a serious obstruction in the way, and there were, on Monday last, thirty-three men engaged in cutting through. Those of our readers who are not acquainted with the nature of rocks, must not suppose that because this is called "rotten" it is therefore easily cut through it. On the other hand, it is more difficult than ordinary rock, in as much as it is much tougher, and, being more porous, the powder used for blasting, when fired, (we were told), "loses itself in it," and thus is less affected than in solid rocks, therefore causing much more manual labour.

While we were present on the spot, the rock was blasted in five different places. As soon as the preliminaries were ready, and the fire applied, all the men turned out, one of their number vigorously blowing the horn, which we understood as an exhortation to everyone it might concern to get out of the reach of danger, and accordingly we followed the navvies in their retreat to an adjoining field. We had scarcely distanced the spot more than a hundred yards before the explosions took place, and scattered large and small pieces of the rock in every direction, for a considerable distance. This being over, all returned, and we observed that huge pieces of the rock had been loosened, and that after the explosion, three trucks were brought up close to the place and loaded. When they were filled they were drawn by horses along rails laid down for temporary use a distance of three hundred yards, where their contents were "keiled up" to carry on

GWR 'Dukedog' 4-4-0 9016 with a Down Goods in the rock cutting just south of Pant station, the site mentioned in the quote from the Advertiser on these pages

an embankment required for the construction of the line. From the spot where this embankment terminates, there intervenes a space of about a hundred yards when the embankment is again made up to the height required for the present purposes of the line.

In the space of a hundred yards, about a dozen stonemasons were at work, erecting a bridge, under which the tram road, used for the conveyance of stone from the rocks above, to the canal, would have to pass [*this is around Pant Station*]. Some men were also engaged in covering a culvert, (for carrying off the water from the copper-washing carried on close by), over which the line would go. After this space, as we stated, the embankment is again made up a considerable distance – probably about a hundred yards, but on this embankment no rails are laid down. There were a dozen men at work here, carrying material from a rock that had been cut through, to both ends, and thus extending the length of it both ways.

Lower down again was another gang of men at work – also about twelve in number – cutting through some earthwork, nearer to Oswestry, and wheeling it to the Llanymynech end of the embankment they had formed, to make up the breach between themselves and the gang higher up. The

A photograph taken in the early 1900s, showing perhaps the most difficult portion of the entire Oswestry & Newtown Railway's works: the cuttings, embankments, and bridges over the road and canal near Well House, Pant. The photographer is standing by the five (or six) kilns. See page 128 for how the bridge on the right looks now (Mrs M Ashton collection)

distance of embankments formed, we should estimate at about a quarter of a mile; and when the three portions are joined, which we should imagine will be done this week, the whole length will form a sight very gratifying to the vision of a shareholder of the Oswestry and Newtown Railway. We may mention that, before the permanent rails are laid down, it will be necessary yet to cover the line with a coating of ballast, which is usually about three feet thick.

In addition to the works above alluded to, preparations have been made for commencing the viaduct required at Llanymynech [*the bridge over the River Vyrnwy*]. It may interest some to know that the wages paid the men vary from 2s 4d to 2s 6d per day, a large majority having to rest satisfied with the former sum. We were rather surprised to hear that figure quoted so low, as it was always our impression that men as able-bodied as navvies, were worth considerably more money. A number of the regular navvies left on Monday morning, owing to the lowness of the wages, and those that remained seemed to express grave dissatisfaction with the pay, stating that they were scarcely able to live, as they have to pay for lodgings, and were charged a high price of everything. We sincerely hope the contractors will not allow any delay of the works on this score.

At the same time, there were meetings in October for an Oswestry, Ellesmere, and Whitchurch Railway, because the ambitious people of the area were already imagining a railway going from Manchester to Milford Haven, via Whitchurch, Oswestry, Llanymynech, Newtown, Llanidloes, and through to Pembrokeshire.

The Llanidloes and Newtown Railway was finished in January 1858, but work was so slow on the Oswestry and Newtown Railway that a meeting took place in December 1857, where the directors announced that they had settled with (ie fired) the contractors Thornton & McCormack, and replaced them with Davidson & Oughterson. But in April 1858, six months after their last progress report, the Advertiser said:

With reference to the rock of the Pant, we regret to say it is not yet got through. Of course the work is very difficult and tedious, and will necessarily take some weeks yet. It is now about two-thirds through, and there are constantly employed at it about sixty men. At Llanymynech a cutting is being very actively worked, and men are employed in taking in the land necessary for station accommodation, and other purposes required at this place.

Most of our readers will be aware that the construction of the bridge over the Verniew [*the River Vyrnwy - or properly Afon Efyrnwy - was spelt, and pronounced, in many different ways*], will be no slight task. It has begun some time ago, and is now being proceeded with as rapidly as possible. The foundations, as we have before stated, are driven with piles, on the top of which concrete is placed, on which the abutments and pillars are built. There are to be three large cast iron cylinders (of great strength), in each of the river pillars or abutments; most of these cylinders have arrived on the spot. The wrought iron girders required are, we believe, finished, and will soon be brought to the place. One of the abutments is now completely, and presents a very handsome appearance.

Altogether we can say, the works are being carried on in a manner every way satisfactory. The promptness with which the contractors have hitherto proceeded must convince the shareholders that nothing will be wanting on their part, to complete the long delayed construction of this line. We only regret, that the land required, cannot always be placed at their disposal as soon as it is required.

Two weeks later there was a description of "a trip by railway" when two 'honest lads' made a journey from Oswestry to Llanymynech on a pony:

We reached Llanymynech very hot and very tired, so much so that one makes signs of distress and put in to the Lion for refreshment. This little episode over we make on for the river, and there really and truly do we see a Railway Bridge in the course of erection.

When we arrive at the works the men are at dinner, but in a few minutes the Church clock strikes one, and they jump up as though they had all been struck, apparently none the worse for an early dinner and a nap in the roasting sun. Most of them are engaged upon the abutments, some dressing the large blocks of stone, and others hoisting one to its place in the "main quoin" with a crane and an apparatus resembling a huge pair of scissors. One of us produces a pencil and pocketbook, for the purpose of taking observations, and the navvy pointing to an elderly individual who stands "taking it easy" with his arms upon the abutments, says "take his picture, sir." As, however, our narrative is not to be illustrated we cannot comply with his request, and proceed to take such notes as we think can be made interesting to the public.

The Llanymynech Bridge will be a wrought iron girder bridge of three spans. This form of construction is generally superseding that of cast iron girders, on account of the superior power of wrought iron to resist extension, and its consequent applicability to large spans, while from the girders being composed of plates riveted together they may be conveyed in parts to the place of erection and put together there. The width of the river where the bridge crosses is not great, but as freshets [a flood from a sudden thaw] are of frequent occurrence, it has been thought expedient to extend the arches some distance beyond its ordinary limits. The principle upon which the piers are being constructed is interesting. Your readers have, doubtless, noticed at the [Oswestry] Railway Station several immense tubes, about the size of a small parlour, and hazarded speculations as to their

The original bridge over the River Vyrnwy at Llanymynech, showing the 'pipes' that formed the piers of the bridge

destination. They were evidently neither drainage, water supply, nor agricultural "pipes." Well, then, these are to form the piers of the new bridge. The bed of the river being a loose shifting gravel, was too yielding in its nature to admit of the ordinary modes of construction, and recourse has been made to the following plan: – Large hollow cylinders of a partially conical form, about 9 feet in diameter at the bottom, and 7 feet at top, are lowered by travelling cranes and between guide piles into the bed of the river until they find "some solid ground to rest upon."

They are provided with flanges on the inner edges, and as they descend, regular cylinders of 7 feet diameter are bolted onto them. They are made to descend either by simple gravity – the ground in interior being excavated so to allow them to descend by their own weight, – or they are forced down by atmospheric pressure.

But there were still financial difficulties with the Oswestry and Newtown Railway. £20,000 of available funds was released, to enable the company to use their borrowing powers to the extent of £80,000 more. There was a hope in July, 1858, that the first portion of the line to Llanymynech would be opened in September, and to Welshpool three or four months later. But then came the Oswestry and Newtown Engineer's report to the directors, on July 31, 1858:

Gentleman, – On the subject of progress of the works, I beg to report, that operations at present are limited to the construction of the portion of the line between Oswestry and the River Severn at Pool Quay, a length

of twelve miles, and to getting in the foundations of the Severn bridges
at Pool Quay and Buttington. On the length between Oswestry and Pool
Quay, the earthwork has made considerable progress – the heavy limestone cutting at Llanymynech being nearly completed, and most of the
other cuttings being either cleared out or in a forward state.
The bridges, both under and over the line, are in a forward state of
progress, and many of them are completed in a sound and satisfactory
manner. The principal bridge on this part of the line is that over the
River Virnew [*Vyrnwy*]; of this, both abutments are finished, the two river
piers brought up above ordinary floodwater height, and the wrought iron
girders are made, and on the ground ready for using.
A considerable portion of the line is ready for ballasting and laying the
permanent way, and nearly two miles of the way is laid. The works are
proceeding under arrangements which had me to expect the above named
lengths (12 miles) being ready for opening by Christmas this year.
Your obedient servant, – Joseph Cubitt.
In August there was a long complaint from Llanymynech in the Advertiser:
As the works draw towards completion, another matter is brought very
prominently before the minds of the interested public – that is, the where-
abouts of the stations. We are given to understand that the desire has
been expressed to have a first-class station at Llandysilio instead of Llanymynech. Such a step, however advantageous it may be to Llandysilio, is
very likely to prove injurious to the best interests of the Railway Company,
in as much as the amount of business transacted at Llanymynech is much
greater than at Llandysilio. There is no comparison between the commer-
cial importance of the two places, the amount paid by Llanymynech alone
for freight and tonnage on the canal being as six to one over and above
that paid by Llandysilio – viz., £300 to £50 – exclusive of the mineral
traffic, which would form a very important item of revenue upon your
line, and for which a large station would be absolutely necessary. There are
also three very important fairs held at Llanymynech, at which there are
frequently from eight to ten thousand sheep penned, as well as pigs, cattle,
and horses, in very large numbers; whereas at Llandysilio there is no fair.
The important districts of Llanfyllin, Meifod, Llanfechain, and Llansantffraid, are the same distance from Llanymynech as Llandysilio, but parties
travelling on your line from these localities will be entirely those who go
towards Oswestry (their market town), Liverpool, Manchester, etc, who
by going to a station at Llanymynech will save themselves one mile and a
half. Again, the inhabitants of Knockin, Kinnerley, Melverley, and Maesbrook, would not travel upon your line if the station were not at Llanymynech, as it would be more convenient for them to go to Oswestry in
their own conveyances. Again, the accommodation as regards inns is far

superior at Llanymynech, and this we think an important consideration for the convenience of the public. The Llanymynech and Burlton trustees of the turnpike road are expending a large sum upon the road, to make the approach to the station as good as possible. Taking these few observations into consideration, it is hoped, for the interests of your line as well as the accommodation of the public, our petition will meet with your most serious and favourable consideration, and that your honourable board will afford a first-class station at Llanymynech.

There was a reply two weeks later, from a 'correspondent', asking who wrote the letter, wondering "why he knew what the people of the district wanted, so much better than they did themselves?"

The Llanymynech Railway

In November 1858, before the Oswestry and Newtown Railway was completed, a plan was put before Parliament for the Llanymynech Railway. This standard gauge line would have replaced the narrow gauge tramways down Llanymynech Hill to the canal, twisted round the present playing fields, and curved into Llanymynech station. The engineer was to have been George Owen, the man who introduced Thomas Savin to David Davies. The Llanfyllin branch was approved instead, and the Llanymynech railway wasn't built, perhaps luckily, because standard gauge tracks full of limestone on an inclined plane can easily go out of control, and might have destroyed most of the English side of the village.

Despite the optimism that the line to Llanymynech would be opened in September 1858, by October 1859 no further progress had been made. At that point the contractors David Davies of Llandinam and Thomas Savin, formerly a draper of Oswestry, were called in, as they had managed to finish the Llanidloes to Newtown Railway. They had the energy and confidence to complete the line. They started immediately on the line that was to be shared with the Shrewsbury and Welshpool Railway, the section from Buttington to Welshpool. They reported to the directors of the Oswestry and Newtown Railway in February 1860:

We hope to open 20 miles of the railway in the spring of the present year, notwithstanding a delay of several months, owing to the unusually wet season, and believe the whole line will be completed before the close of the year. 12 miles of your railway may be said to be ready for opening, and the necessary rolling stock has been brought on your property.

The Porthywaen branch

Also in February 1860 there was a proposal for a branch railway, one which shows the rivalry between the old tramways and the new standard gauge railways:
On Wednesday last, the proposed Llynckliss [Llynclys] branch of the Oswestry and Newtown Railway passed the examiners as having complied with the standing orders. The branch will join the mainline at Llynckliss, and terminates near the lime kilns at Porthywaen.
In the next month at the hearing for the proposal of the branch line from Llynclys to the lime rocks at Porthywaen, the bill was opposed by the owners of the Crickheath tramway, the Misses Newill, but they were defeated and the proposal approved.

OSWESTRY AND NEWTOWN RAILWAY.

Bankers' Receipt.

Fourth Call of £2 per Share, making £9 paid.

No. 76 Number of Shares 20 — — — Distinguishing Numbers.

From 1051 to 1070 inclusive.

Received the 19 day of May 1858.

from Thos S Dickin Esq. Rep.

on Account of the Oswestry and Newtown Railway Company, the sum of Forty

Pounds, being the fourth Call of £2 per Share, upon Twenty Shares in the Capital of the

Company.

For

£. s. d.

Principal 40

Interest

Total 40

ABOVE *An 1858 receipt for the purchase of O&N Shares*

BELOW *A very early photo of the station at Llanymynech, around 1870, showing some of the staff, as well as passengers. The track coming in from the left is the original layout for the Potts Railway, before the track was relaid to the south of the down platform (Mrs E Evans collection)*

The grand beginning

THE OPENING OF THE OSWESTRY & NEWTOWN RAILWAY

At last, in April 1860, a government inspector went over the line from Oswestry to Pool Quay, and "he expressed himself very much pleased with the line generally." In May, the first locomotive, "The Montgomery, with a number of trucks with rough seats placed on them for the occasion, went from Oswestry to Welshpool. The train was brought to a standstill on the very spot where, some years ago, we are afraid to say how many, the first sod was cut. In Welshpool the bells rung out merry peals, and cannons were fired, and everything betokened the hilarity of the inhabitants. There is every reason to hope that in a very few weeks we will see in Welshpool a terminus."

In fact it had been almost 3 years and three sets of contractors before the line from Oswestry to Welshpool was opened, an unusually long time in those railway building days for a mere 16 miles.

At the opening, on August 14, 1860, "on the line of railway, several decorations were made. The engines and the stations were all ornamented with streamers, flags, and laurel. At Pool Quay, a large arch spanned the line; at Llandysilio and Llanymynech, similar arches were erected, and decorations in profusion prevailed. We must not forget to mention that the station buildings at Llanymynech were ornamented by the family at the rectory, aided by Mr Deam, painter. The flags and banners of the several clubs added much to the appearance.

In June 1861 the Oswestry to Newtown Railway was approved by the inspectors, and locomotives began to run from Oswestry through Llanymynech to Llanidloes.

Early accident

This was an early accident on the Oswestry to Newtown Railway:

Accident. – On Monday last an accident occurred on the Oswestry and Newtown Railway, to a young man named Edward Thomas, which might have resulted fatally, had not great exertions been made to remove him at once from his precarious position. It appears that he and several other men were loading some large timber at Llanymynech, when one of the trees overpowered them, knocked Thomas down, and fell upon his breast. He was speedily conveyed to Oswestry by an engine, when, by the orders of Mr Savin, one of the contractors, he was placed under the care of Dr Fuller. He now lies in a dangerous state.

From the Advertiser, January 1860

Assault

This was an early misdemeanour on the Oswestry to Newtown Railway:

Assault. – Thomas Morris was charged with assaulting Mr Billinge, stationmaster, Llynclys. Defendant said he did not remember anything about it. Mr Billinge proved the case, and said the defendant had come to Llynclys station with an insufficient ticket, and refused to give up his ticket, or pay the excess, and that when he demanded it, hit him with all his force. He afterwards paid the fare. Defendant said he was very sorry, he had been receiving his pension that day in Welshpool, and spent too long a time in drinking the Queen's health with his old comrades. Fined 10s, and costs.

From the Advertiser, November 1862

Negligence on the railways

Here is an example of the penalties given for negligence on the railways:

At the Oswestry County police court, on Saturday, James Fairbanks, engine driver, and James Owen, pointsman, were charged with negligently causing an accident to occur on the Oswestry and Newtown Railway, on the 28th January. The facts of the case were these. – A few minutes after seven o'clock on the night in question, the passenger train for Oswestry was leaving the Llanymynech station, and had proceeded about a quarter of a mile, when it came into collision with a ballast engine, and both engines were thrown off the rails, but no one was seriously injured. The collision occurred at the points, and it was alleged by the prosecutor that both Fairbanks, the driver of the ballast engine, and Owen, the pointsman, were guilty of negligence, but that Owen was far more guilty than the other defendant, because Fairbanks was a younger hand and took his engine on the mainline at the order of Owen. It appeared from the evidence that the ballast engine ought not to have been shunting within a quarter of an hour of the time the passenger train was due, but that Owen, who, a few minutes before, had received a ticket for the driver of the other engine, ordered Fairbanks to fetch some waggons from a siding, and Fairbanks was in the act of executing this order when the accident occurred. The charge against Fairbanks was dismissed, but Owen was sentenced to 14 days' imprisonment with hard labour.

From the Advertiser, February 1863

A trip on the light fantastic

THE LLANFYLLIN RAILWAY

While the Oswestry to Newtown railway was being built, the small market town of Llanfyllin was determined it would be connected to the railway network. A meeting was held at Llanfyllin Town Hall on October 13, 1860. The West Midlands, Shrewsbury and Coast of Wales Railway sent representatives, because their intention was to build a railway from Shrewsbury to Llanymynech, Llanfyllin, through the Berwyn hills and across to Dolgellau. But the people of Llanfyllin thought that a more realistic option was a branch from Llanymynech. This was agreed, after the estimate of the cost was made at about £60,000. A year later, when the money had been raised by subscription, the ceremony of Cutting the First Sod of the Llanfyllin railway was performed.

> Llanymynech was out for a holiday on the arrival of the trains from Oswestry and Welshpool, and vehicles of all descriptions, and some that beggar description were put in requisition to convey visitors to Llanfyllin. Three or four of those hard-working men who do so much for their "fellow's speeches", were unfortunate in getting no vehicles at all, and had to fall back upon the primitive conveyance of shank's ponies, which carried them in safety as far as Llansantffraid, and while they rested, basking in the sun, their owners had time to make a note of the manner in which the inhabitants of that spirited little village commemorated the day.
>
> *From the Advertiser, September 25, 1861*

The contractor was Thomas Savin, in partnership with his brother-in-law John Ward and engineer Benjamin Piercy, and they quickly built the line. It was 9¼ miles in length, and there were few problems. The strange thing was that the line passed close to Llanymynech limeworks and quarry, and met the Oswestry and Newtown Railway half a mile north of Llanymynech, after a steep gradient to go over the Shropshire Union Canal. This meant that trains from Llanfyllin had to join the main line, and reverse down into a bay platform at Llanymynech, before going back the same way to Oswestry. The reason given for this very awkward arrangement was that the West Shropshire Mineral Railway had had approval for a line that went south and west from Llanymynech

station (which after 1896 was used by the Llanfyllin branch). But I doubt it is a coincidence that the arrangement meant that the limeworks, owned by Thomas Savin, were now very conveniently placed near a standard gauge railway line. The first locomotive ran from Llanymynech on September 20, 1862.

By steam to Llansantffraid!

The Llanfyllin Railway may safely be said to be the most wonderful of the projects of this nature that has hitherto seen the light in this district. It has no rock cutting, like the Newtown and Machynlleth one at Talerddig; no Moss, like the one on the Ellesmere and Whitchurch line at Whixall; indeed, no engineering difficulties at all, yet it is a wonder of wonders, for – it was allowed to passed through Parliament unopposed! Thanks to the genius of Mr Piercy and Mr Savin, the line was projected, passed, and the works commenced, and the works have so far progressed, that on Saturday last inhabitants of Llansantffraid saw what mortal man never saw before, to wit, a locomotive drive right into the village.

The course of the line, as our readers probably know, is over the canal from the north side of Llanymynech station, to the turnpike road just above the village, under which it runs, and along the valley until it reaches the Tanat, which is crossed by a pile-bridge just below Gravel Hill; from thence, following the course of the river, to the village of Llansantffraid. We understand it is intended to open the line so far for goods traffic, on the 1st October, which will be a great boon to the people of the district, as it will tend considerably reduce the price of coal and lime, and the amount of "team" labour. The line further on is a very forward state; the fencing for some miles been completed, and the works actively commenced.

From the Advertiser, September 24, 1862

The line was opened officially on July 17, 1863, and Thomas Savin arranged a train to the seaside for local people. 600 people turned up at Llanfyllin, Llansanffraid and Llanymynech stations for the trip:

Opening of the Llanfyllin Railway

The celebration of the opening of the line took place on Friday, and the committee of management adopted a very sensible and pleasant way of inaugurating the introduction of the locomotive, by taking a trip to the seaside. The Oswestry and Newtown Company provided twenty-three carriages and Llanfyllin filled with every variety of passengers. There were some who had never been on a railway before, others who had never seen a sheet of water bigger than a mill pool, and not a few who had never before accomplished so lengthy a journey.

The newly-popular Borth was the watering place fixed upon, and soon after seven o'clock in the morning about 600 of the good folks of Llanfyllin set out from their station en route for that delightful local town. The incidents of the journey were few. The rules of the company regarding smoking were not strictly observed by the passengers; and the promises of the company that the train should arrive at Borth at 10.45 were not fulfilled; but nobody was the worst for this.

Arrived at Borth, the excursionists followed the bent of their own inclination. Mr Maddocks's refreshment rooms were of course filled in five minutes; the splendid sands were dotted upon with people in five more, and speedily the bathing machines and the pleasure boats were put into active operation. The train started punctually at half past one in returning, and arrived at Llanfyllin at about half past five o'clock. The bells of the parish church rang merrily during the whole of the day, and the Llanymynech Brass Band paraded the streets playing several lively airs, and for a short time they played, while some who delighted therein, enjoyed on the green near the station, a trip on the "light fantastic toe."

Accident on the Llanfyllin Railway

There was an accident to Jack Morgan, the Huntsman of the Tanat-side Harriers: The particulars of poor Jack's end are very tragic. It appears that since the opening of the Llanfyllin branch railway he has often been in the habit of crossing the Grove Bridge, just above the point where the Tanat empties itself into the Vyrnwy, in order to save himself two miles walking from the kennels to the place of meeting; and on Tuesday evening, when returning with the hounds to the kennels, a passing engine ran into the midst of the pack, slaughtering eight or nine of the hounds, and, as it afterwards appeared, knocking poor Jack into the river. The body was not found until Friday night, when it was dragged out of the Vyrnwy, nearly a mile from the Grove Bridge. From the evidence it appeared that Morgan had been seen running down the line (which is very steep at that point), in the direction of the bridge; and that at the time the wind was so high that it is supposed he would be unable to hear the train coming along. The driver too, stated that he did not see the dogs until he was in the midst of the pack, and that he did not see the man at all. When the body was found, it was sadly mutilated, the ribs under the left arm being completely smashed, and the right leg broken in two places. It is a somewhat singular fact, that just at the point where the deceased's hunting cap was found, one of the timbers forming the fence at the side of the bridge had been knocked out for some time, and through this open space the body must been thrown into the water whence it was carried away by the current, which was very strong at the time. Jack Morgan, although only sixty years of age, had been associated with the Tanat side harriers for half a century, and it was only on the previous Thursday that he had been congratulated on his long service, by the gentlemen of the hunt, at their annual dinner.

From the Advertiser, March 1865

Amalgamation
THE CAMBRIAN RAILWAYS

The Oswestry, Ellesmere, and Whitchurch Railway opened in May, 1863, and in June a bill was promoted by the Oswestry and Newtown, the Llanidloes and Newtown, the Oswestry, Ellesmere, and Whitchurch, and the Newtown and Machynlleth Companies, to amalgamate the four companies into one, under the name of "The Cambrian Railways Company."

Not everyone was happy with the new railway. There was an early complaint about the lack of speed in this letter of January 1868 to the Editor of the Advertiser:

Travelling by the Cambrian railway

Sir, – Last Monday week my son and I went to Welshpool, he on horseback, I by rail. When we were returning he accompanied me to the station, and then went uptown, got his horse ready, and rode to Oswestry, where he arrived sometime before my train, which had started first.

Yours,

A traveller

The Cambrian Railways were never a hugely successful enterprise. The rural areas they served suffered depopulation during the sixty years of the Cambrian's existence. They never completed their Manchester to Milford Haven

Cambrian Railways 4-4-0 No 60, built May 1891, at Llanymynech, about 1905

The station at Llanymynech in 1904, cattle trucks in the bay platform

line. The directors were hauled before the Houses of Parliament for breach of privilege, when a Station Master, John Hood, complained about the long hours men had to work (sometimes as much as 36 continuous hours).

During the First World War there was a tremendous burst of traffic, as coal from South Wales went north to Scapa Flow for the Royal Navy fleet, and the coal trains passed through Llanymynech.

Then there was the Abermule disaster in 1921, the most famous and terrible accident on a single line, when two trains, one an express train from Aberystwyth to London and Manchester (it used to divide at Welshpool) and the local train from Whitchurch to Aberystwyth, collided head-on – an accident primarily caused by the driver and fireman not reading the name on the tablet that was meant to make single line working foolproof. It made the Cambrian Railways famous in a way no railway company wanted. The next year they were taken over, with most of the other Welsh railway companies, by the Great Western Railway.

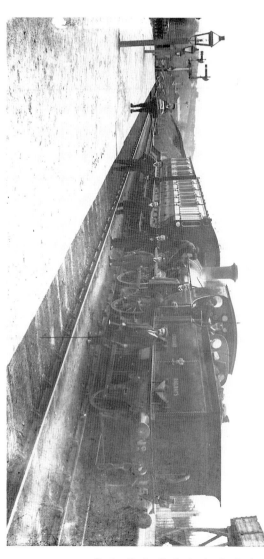

LEFT In the early 1900s, Cambrian Railways 0-6-0 No 15 Glansevern, built September 1875 by Sharp, Stewart & Co (formerly Sharp, Roberts & Co, co-founded by Richard Roberts of Llanymynech), is on the down platform at Llanymynech with the Llanyblodwel train. The track had been changed from the way it was in the photo on page 18, the Potts line now met the Cambrian line south of the down platform

BELOW An official Cambrian photograph, probably in August 1902, of 4-4-0 No 19, with a completely Oswestry built train, nine coaches, everything newly out of the works (though the tender did not belong to 19) at a siding at Llanymynech. In the background, above the tender, is the bridge that took Rock Siding over the canal. On the extreme right can just be seen the large warehouse that stood at the neck of the Oswestry to Welshpool and Llanymynech to Llanfyllin lines

ABOVE *Cambrian Railways No 66 heading south to Welshpool, at Llanymynech signal box (F Fox-Davies)*

BELOW *The staff of Llanymynech station in 1917 – a large number of males considering the size of the station and the fact that the First World War was in full flow – including Mr Ebenezer Davies, the Station Master (presumably centre of the middle row)*

The Grand Lunatic Railway
THE WEST SHROPSHIRE MINERAL RAILWAY

Another new railway:
"We shall next hear of a Railway to the Moon, or to Llansilin," said a
gentleman of our acquaintance, two years ago, when he was told of the
sundry wild goose chases, engineers proposed to take over, through, and
round the Berwyn. There is many a true word spoken in jest, and although
neither of these places is actually to be touched by the schemes of 1862-
3, still one of them is closely passed. On this occasion the lines are to go
nearer Llansilin than the Moon, but who knows in another year or two we
may have a Grand Lunatic railway in the market!

So far, however, our engineers have kept to terra firma, and content themselves with an approach to the Berwyn Mountain. Our readers are aware
that during the last session, a company called the "West Shropshire Mineral" obtained the sanction of Parliament for making a line from Yockleton station on the Shrewsbury and Welshpool railway, to Llanymynech.
The promoters of this project are now seeking to continue the line from
Llanymynech, to Llanrhaeadr and Llangynog. This is the chief feature of

*The timber bridge of the Potts Railway over the River Tanat near the weir at Carreghofa Hall.
Presumably when the line had crossed North Wales and was a main line, this bridge would
have been replaced with something more suitable*

the one scheme. The other, which is called the "Oswestry and Llangynog Railway," is to be a continuation of the existing Porthywaen branch of the Oswestry and Newtown, to the same places.

From the Advertiser of November 16, 1862

Fantastically grandiose schemes and simple practical plans often clashed in Victorian railway projects, but they came together in the line that was built between Shrewsbury and Llanymynech and on to Nantmawr. On the one hand was the desire to cross North Wales to a port on the coast for Dublin, and this ambition can still be seen in the wide bridges, for example at Wern Junction near Carreghofa School, or a mile out of Llanymynech on the road to Shrewsbury, or the abutments of the bridge across the Tanat at Carreghofa Hall. Clearly the intention was a double track mainline from Shrewsbury to Llangynog and across to the Welsh coast. On the other hand, RS France wanted a mineral line for his limestone quarries at Nantmawr, and he got one, but the suspicion has to be that he tempted investors with the idea of a grand line to Ireland in order to get it.

When Brunel and the Great Western Railway's scheme to go across to Wales from Shrewsbury was abandoned when the London & North Western Railway opened the North Wales coast route to Holyhead, a new Bill was introduced in Parliament in 1861: the West Midlands, Shrewsbury and Coast of Wales Railway. The bill was rejected, but a new plan started, the West Shropshire Mineral Railway, a suitably realistic title for a line from Yockleton near Westbury to Llanymynech. This was promoted by RS France, the secretary of the Mid Wales Railway, and owner of quarries around Llanymynech and Nantmawr. But as the ideas became grander the name changed, to the Shrewsbury and North Wales Railway, to go from Shrewsbury across the Severn at Shrawardine to Llanymynech. There would be two branches, one to Criggion Quarry for the granite (this quarry is of course still worked), and one beyond Llanymynech to the Nantmawr limestone quarries.

There was some progress, at least with the surveying, as shown in this letter of February 26, 1863:

Engineer's report to the Directors of the West Shropshire Mineral Railway
Gentlemen, I have the honour to report that the permanent survey of your railway, from the junction with the Oswestry and Newtown Railway at Llanymynech, to the river Severn, at Shrawardine, has been completed, a considerable portion of the land has been purchased, and the whole as between Llanymynech and Shrawardine will shortly be in possession of the contractor, who is proceeding rapidly with the fencing. A large portion of the permanent way is in course of delivery, and the works on the length before mentioned will be carried out at once.
I have the honour to remain, Gentlemen,
Your obedient servant, John Ashdown

This was all still quite realistic, but then the North Staffordshire Railway stepped in. They wanted to link the Potteries with Shrewsbury, and the Shrewsbury and North Wales Railway suggested they join together for a line from Stoke-on-Trent to Shrewsbury, across to Llanymynech, to Llanyblodwel, Llangynog, and across the mountains to Porthmadog, to go to Ireland. This was the Potts Railway.

The Meifod Valley Railway

Meanwhile, in November 1865 there was another plan, one which came to nothing:

Amongst the other schemes of the coming session, one which interests some of our readers, is a proposal by Mr France to make a railway up the Meifod Valley. The proposed line will commence in the parish of Llanymynech, by a junction with the Shrewsbury and North Wales railway, and, passing up the Meifod Valley, will terminate near Llanfair vicarage.

From the Advertiser, November 1, 1865

The bridge under the canal and B4398 near Carreghofa School, the site of the accident described on the next page (though this picture was taken after 1896, when the spur to the right had been built). See page 105 for the present but unchanged and rather magnificent underside of the bridge

Accident on the Shrewsbury and North Wales Railway

The report of this death at Llanymynech states it was in the building of the Llangynog line. In fact it was the line from Llanymynech to Llanyblodwel and Nantmawr, but it shows that the clear intention was to go to Llangynog. The accident seems to have happened in the cutting under and around the canal at Carreghofa, and shows the dangerous methods of the navvies. To make it easier to remove large amounts of earth they would undermine the rock, allowing it to fall, but occasionally this happened, from the Advertiser of June 8, 1865:

Two men killed by a fall of earth

On Thursday last Peter Robinson and Samuel Jones, two navvies in the employ of Mr France, were killed in the earth works of the Llangynog line, near Llany-mynech. An inquest was held at the Dolphin Inn.

Samuel Morris said – I'm a labourer working on the Shrewsbury and North Wales Railway. Both of the deceased worked in the (continued on next page) same gang. We were all yesterday employed removing soil, from a cutting near Mr Sockett's. I was what is called the getter and the deceased with another man were filling. I was engaged getting down a fall of earth when the deceased both came up and began to fill soil from opposite the fall. I called to them to look out, for that it was not to be trusted. They however brought up a waggon and began to fill it and I then assisted them. I suddenly saw the soil was coming down when I called out "look up." I escaped but cannot tell how I did. The earth then fell in a considerable quantity. When I escaped I looked for the deceased and found both of the deceased were under the soil. Samuel Jones was cov-ered all beside his head. Peter Robinson was partially covered. It may have been from five to ten minutes before we got them from under the soil. Samuel Jones breathed, I believe, once or twice. Before we were able to remove the soil, Peter Robinson said two or three times, "Oh, good men, get it off me, get me loose." We were all so frightened I hardly knew what occurred. The doctor ar-rived almost directly but before his arrival both men were dead. I often thought the deceased men were not sufficiently cautious and that they would not heed a caution.

This accident happened at Carreghofa, on the same line and near the place of the previous accident, just six months later:

Fatal accident. – On Monday Pryce Williams, of Treflach, one of a number of men engaged in ballasting at Carreghofa, met with his death in the following manner: – Whilst foolishly trying to jump on the ballast trucks (to save the walk of ten or twelve yards) his foot slipped, and he fell on the rails. The train passed over him, nearly cutting off his legs. He was carried on a shutter to Llanymynech station, and thence conveyed via Buttington to Shrewsbury infirmary, but he died almost immediately on his arrival there.

Fantasy & reality

THE POTTERIES, SHREWSBURY AND NORTH WALES RAILWAY

The Potteries, Shrewsbury and North Wales Railway, usually shortened to the Potts, was an amalgamation on July 16 1866 of the Shrewsbury and North Wales Railway, the successor to the West Shropshire Midland Railway, and the Shrewsbury and Potteries Junction Railway.

One problem the Potts had was that the Great Western Railway and London & North Western Railway, who jointly owned Shrewsbury station, felt threatened by the new scheme, and insisted that the Potts would not use their station. So a new Shrewsbury station was built, by the Abbey, called Abbey Foregate Station, and a magnificent double track line was laid from there to Llanymynech. The fact that a line that went through the quiet country between Shrewsbury and Llanymynech (which had a population of about 1000 people) had two tracks showed the hopeless lack of realism of its builders, especially as west of Llanymynech they got no further than Llanyblodwel on their way to Ireland. In fact, at a cost of £60,000 a mile to construct it was said to be the most expensive non-metropolitan railway in the country.

Nevertheless, on August 13, 1866, the Potteries, Shrewsbury and North Wales Railway opened between Shrewsbury Abbey Foregate and Llanymynech. It didn't last the year. 1866 was the year of financial collapses. Thomas Savin went bust in February, owing £2 million. In May Overend and Gurney collapsed, the last British bank to do so till Northern Rock in 2007. RS France had bankruptcy proceedings against him the day after the opening of the Potts Railway. The bailiffs moved in, and seized the train from Shrewsbury to Llanymynech.

The Potts station building at Llanymynech. It didn't change very much over the next 100 years (see page 120) (F Fox-Davies)

The Manchester Guardian reported "it being fair day in Shrewsbury, and a large number of passengers from the several stations along the line having taken return tickets, much inconvenience to the public was likely to ensue. The North Wales section of the line was completed in August last, at a cost of a little over £1,100,000." There is also a famous story of a carriage being uncoupled and left at Kinnerley with a bailiff in it, so he had to walk back to Shrewsbury (see On the Border). A receiver was appointed and the railway closed on December 21, 1866. There was a report in the Advertiser that there was an advertisement in the Railway Times, announcing the sale of the engines and other rolling stock.

Two years later, and after some financial consolidation, the line reopened, officially on December 28, 1868, though the Advertiser already had this report on November 4:

> Mr France's railway. – The Shrewsbury and North Wales Railway, from Llanymynech to Shrewsbury, was reopened for traffic on Saturday. This will be a great boon to the farmers who attend Oswestry and Shrewsbury markets.

The service was reduced. It had been five trains a day each way, and it was now three. The track was reduced to a single line, but the most the railway made in the year was a few hundred pounds, after an investment of over a million pounds. The journey was slow, and though the passenger figures improved

Another Potts station, this time at Llanyblodwell (so called), later renamed Blodwell Junction. It shows a Potteries Railway slotted signal

slightly, a receiver was appointed again in 1877. Three years later a passenger complained about the state of Melverley bridge, the Board of Trade inspected the railway and discovered the track and bridges were in a terrible state. The Potts couldn't afford to put it right, so on 19 June 1880 the line closed again.

The Cambrian Railways agreed to take over the branch from Llany-mynech via Llanyblodwel to Nantmawr quarries, so RS France managed to keep his quarries served by the railway. The Cambrian Railways paid the Potts receiver 3d for every ton carried on the line, later reduced to 2d a ton.

A new concern, the Shropshire Railways Company, attempted in 1888 to revive the line from Llanymynech to Shrewsbury. They bought the line, cleared it and put new sleepers and fences down, but after less than a year, and before they could reopen the line, they too went bankrupt.

For the next sixteen years the line was shut. One man, Richard Reeves, an old Potts guard, used to go up and down on a hand propelled trolley, main-taining the fences to keep out cattle. Otherwise, and seemingly forever, the line was dead.

*Typical of the state the Potts got into after it closed: at Maesbrook, over the River Morda,
towards the end of the 19th century (F Fox-Davies)*

Potts assault

This incident happened just before the Potts closed:

Llanymynech - Serious charge against Mr Kinsey.

On Monday, Stephen Kinsey, a respectably dressed man, described as being formally a farmer at Newtown, and now a butcher at Llanymynech, was brought before the Borough Magistrates at Shrewsbury, charged with committing an indecent assault upon a young woman, named Mary Ann Briscoe. The offence was alleged to have been committed on Monday week, in a third class carriage, between Shrewsbury and Ford, on the Shrewsbury, Potteries, and North Wales Railway. From the evidence of the prosecutrix, it appeared that she got into the carriage to travel by the 7.30 p.m. train from Shrewsbury to Ford. There was no one else in the carriage except herself and the prisoner, and he was separated from her by two compartments. Almost before the train started he climbed over the division towards her, and seating himself beside her, commenced a series of assaults upon her person, which continued until she reached Ford, the first station at which the train stopped. As soon as the train slackened speed to stop at Ford, the prosecutrix managed to open the door and jumped out while the train was yet in motion. The prisoner seized hold of her dress to detain her, and she fell onto the platform, and narrowly escaped what might have proved a fatal accident. It was not denied the defendant was guilty of some improprieties, but it was urged in mitigation, that the prisoner was under the influence of drink at the time. It was further mentioned for the defence that the prisoner was a married man, and the father of seven children.

From the Advertiser, November 1866

At the Shrewsbury court sessions, neither Mary Ann Briscoe nor Stephen Kinsey appeared, and it was said that Kinsey had gone to America. Whether he took his wife and seven children with him isn't mentioned.

Sad accident

Sad accident on the Shrewsbury and North Wales line

On Saturday last an old man named William Hughes, in the employ of Mr William Rogers, Llywntidman, met with his death while taking his master's cows to the pasture. Deceased had to cross the line to do so. At the moment of crossing, the train, due at Kinnerley at 4.50 p.m., came up, and knocking the poor fellow down he was killed instantaneously.

From the Advertiser, July 1869

Making their escape

This occurred at Llanymynech Railway Station, rather to the shame of Llany-mynech:

Making their escape. – William Syars, a suspicious character (and tramping tai-lor), was brought up in custody of PC Simcox, and charged with stealing a pair of trousers, the property of Mr Lloyd, Wheelwright, the Pant. The prisoner was remanded till Thursday for further enquiries to be made. It appears that when the officer apprehended Syars he was in company with another man. They were both taken into custody, and were conveyed to Llanymynech Railway Station. Whilst waiting for the train the prisoner Syars slipped the handcuffs and made off. The officer gave chase and captured him, and on returning found that the other prisoner had made his escape with the handcuffs on, the passengers on the platform – much to their discredit – not having made the slightest attempt to stop him.

From the Advertiser, February 1868

Robbery at a railway station

Robbery at a railway station. – At the Town Hall, on Wednesday, David Williams, porter at the Llanymynech station on the Cambrian Railway, was charged by Inspector Thomas, of that company's service, with stealing six yards of calico. A few days previously the stationmaster picked up a parcel upon the platform, and for some time it was unclaimed. When Mr Middleton, late of Morton, sent to enquire about it, the stationmaster went into his office and found that the parcel had been removed. A telegram was sent to Inspector Thomas, requesting him to go to Llanymynech and investigate the case. The inspector suspected the porter of having taken the parcel, and told him that he should search his house. On the road to the house the prisoner admitted that he had the parcel, and reaching home he gave the contents of it up to the inspector. The parcel had been opened, the calico cut in two, and part of it made into a chemise. The pris-oner, on bail, was remanded until tomorrow, when he will be dealt with under the Criminal Justice Act.

The bench, while taking into consideration the previous good character of the prisoner, said it was a case in which the sentence must be severe. Prisoner was left in charge of the place, and he had taken advantage of that opportunity to abstract the parcel out of the office. – The sentence would be four months' imprisonment, with hard labour.

From the Advertiser, October 1869

THE RAILWAYS OF LLANYMYNECH

In 1872 a worker at the limeworks was knocked down by the Llanfyllin to Llanymynech train. There was a strange layout, very near to where the old stables is
now. The tramway crossed the main Llanfyllin to Llanymynech line on the level,
wagons being allowed to run down the gradient and across the line. One wagon,
unnoticed by the foreman, remained on the crossing and blocking the line. The
man in charge of the crossing, John Whittington, tried to push the wagon off
the line as the Llanfyllin train approached. The driver shouted, but Whittington
was hit by the train. When the driver reached Llanymynech station, he told the
inspector, and they went back to see about the man. The rather strange thing
here is that the driver would have had to have travelled half a mile further, after
hitting John Whittington, and reversed down to Llanymynech station before he
did anything about the man his engine had killed.

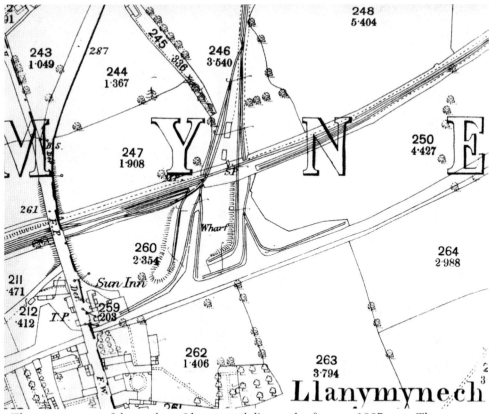

*The arrangement of the tracks at Llanymynech limeworks, from an 1887 map. The tramway
comes from the Hill to the north, over the Llanfyllin main line on the level (at the bottom of the
large Y), and curves into a siding. This is very near the stables of the present heritage area*

The judge and the railway guard
THE SENSATIONAL CASE

This was a rather sensational case of March 1876, the word of a judge versus that of a railway guard in the matter of the weather at Llanymynech – and the guard was right. The editorial in the Advertizer did not pull any punches:

At Llanfyllin County Court last week an opportunity was afforded Mr Homersham Cox, of apologising to the railway guard whom he had unjustly accused of falsehood in the case of "Mills v the Cambrian company," an action for alleged delay in the delivery of cattle, heard the previous October. On that occasion, it will be remembered, the guard, James Thompson, deposed his train was delayed by the weather on 26th of December, 1876, when he found about a foot of snow at Llanymynech; upon which the judge remarked that "he was asked to believe there was a foot of snow at Llanymynech, who must be very innocent to believe such a statement as that. In his opinion there was not a single word of truth in the tale the guard had told about the snow; it was a tissue of falsehoods from beginning to end." One would naturally suppose that the learned judge has some regard to the reputation of those who come before him, and that he happened to know that no snow fell on 26th of December, 1876. But he can have known nothing of the kind. Turning to our diary we find the entry: "1876 – Dec. 26, deep snow." This we pointed out at the time, and expressed an opinion, with which all our readers except Mr Homersham Cox must have agreed, that the learned judge would take the earliest opportunity of clearing the character of the guard and apologising for the serious reflection which be made upon the reputation of a respectable man. To our surprise, Mr Cox showed no desire to withdraw the charge; but we then supposed that he was only waiting until a favourable occasion presented itself for a full explanation of the case and a graceful retirement from the position he had assumed as accuser of Thompson. Such an occasion has now been allowed to pass. Mr Cox has not only refused a new trial, though one of the reasons given for his former decision – that the guard's tale was untrue – is proved to be entirely without foundation, but he has said no word to put the guard right with the public. The newspapers have done that, it is true, but it is difficult to understand Mr Homersham Cox's views of the duties and responsibilities of a judge, to say nothing of the ordinary usages of English gentlemen. It is a serious thing for the public if anyone who is called upon to appear in the witness box, to further the ends of justice, is liable to have his character for veracity, which perhaps he values more than anything else in the world, arbitrarily called in question by the judge himself. In this case, fortunately for Thompson, his character was at once vindicated by incontrovertible facts, but the case can easily be imagined in which a groundless charge could not be so easily disposed of, and in other circumstances Thompson might have received irreparable injury for the baseless charge which was made against him by Mr Cox. The learned judge took notice of the remarks that have been made upon the case, so far as to say that he should require strong evidence before he apologised, but we hope it is usual for English judges to require strong evidence before they charge men with lying. In the interest of the public it is to be hoped the case will not be allowed to rest here. We have confined ourselves to the question of the charge against Thompson, but we cannot profess to understand the mental process by which Mr Cox arrived at his decisions in October and March. In October he denied that there was any snow on the line, and gave a verdict for plaintiff. In March he refuses a new trial, and remarks that if there was snow it was the Company's duty to clear it off. It will occur to most persons that it was probably the process of clearing the line which delayed the train!

The junction officially known as Nantmawr Junction (as the track on the right went to Nantmawr) or locally as Wern junction, because it was at the Wern, Llanymynech (by Carreghofa Halt, and School). This shows the junction after the spur to Llanfyllin, to the left, had been made, but before the signal box between the tracks was built. Note the gate, probably to keep livestock off the track, which shows the state of the Potts at that time. The old Llanfyllin line bridge has been demolished, in the background and this side of the road bridge at Carreghofa Lane. The short ballast siding was removed around 1913 (F Fox-Davies)

SEE NEXT PAGE

The quiet line
THE NANTMAWR BRANCH

The Nantmawr branch between Llanymynech and Nantmawr was kept open and operated by the Cambrian Railways from 1881, and in 1894 they reached an agreement with the Shropshire Railways' receiver to build a short line connecting the Nantmawr branch with the Llanfyllin railway. For over thirty years trains from Llanfyllin joined the main Oswestry to Newtown line a quarter of a mile north of Llanymynech station, and had to reverse down into Llanymynech, before going back along the line to Oswestry. This was inconvenient, and added several minutes onto the journey. Now, with the new deviation opened on January 27, 1896, trains could go from Oswestry to Llanymynech and continue past Llanymynech junction to what was now Nantmawr Junction, and on to Llanfyllin. The half mile line was built by the Cambrian's engineer, George Owen, the man who was going to build the Llanymynech Railway. The new junction had a signal box, and obliterated an old siding from the Nantmawr line to the canal.

The old section of the Llanfyllin branch was used as a siding and loading bay for the limeworks, the part from Carreghofa to just west of the A483 bridge being lifted, the remaining part called Rock Siding and serving Llanymynech limeworks. Three years later the great Hoffmann kiln was built, but this was only in use for a short time, closing on the August Bank Holiday, 1914, as the First World War broke out, and Rock Siding was closed by the Cambrian Railways at the same time (though the rails remained, for the storage of crippled wagons, until the outbreak of World War II).

When the Tanat Valley Light Railway was opened between Llynclys junction and Llangynog on January 5 1904, the Cambrian began a passenger service between Llanymynech and Blodwel Junction (formerly Llanyblodwel, though it was over half a mile from the village; there was a later station nearer the village when the Tanat Valley line opened). This was one of the least used services in the country, with perhaps one passenger in the winter and two or three in the summer. The passenger service stopped during the First World War, on January 1, 1917, though the goods service (one train each way) continued until 1925. The track was slowly lifted, the north part to Blodwell Junction lifted around 1930, the rest between 1936 and 1938, and rumoured to have been sent to be used in France when the Second World War broke out.

OPPOSITE *The layouts at Wern junction, on the left from a map of 1887, before the spur was built, on the right from a map of 1901 with the spur. Note in the 1887 map the siding that came up from Nantmawr and to beside the canal. Perhaps this was so that Mr France could avoid using the Cambrian Railways, and put his limestone onto canal boats instead. The short spurs of the canal were what is left of the diversion that was built when the railway bridge was made, so that the canal could continue to operate during the making of the bridge*

The broken bridge of the old Llanfyllin line, looking south towards the Wern, around 1898
(F Fox-Davies)

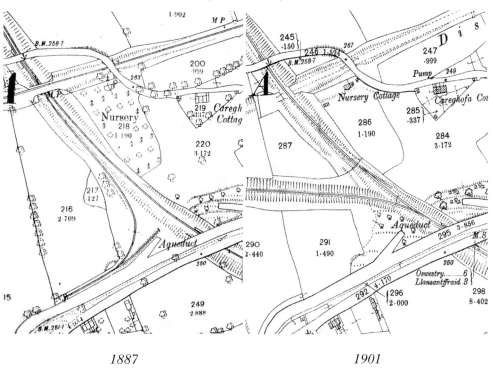

1887   *1901*

ABOVE *A photo of the bridge over the canal at Rock Siding, long after its closure in 1914, the Hoffmann kiln chimney in the background (Lewis Cozens)*

BELOW *The signal box at Nantmawr Junction, opened December 15, 1895. The signalman had so little to do he spent most of his time repairing boots in the box. A few yards of the line to Nantmawr, on the right, was used as a siding for crippled wagons, until re-opened by the Cambrian. To the right of the signal box can be seen the slope of the start of the old siding, that went up to the canal, out of sight on the left, before the spur was built*

A remarkable accident
THE WERN JUNCTION ACCIDENT

On 7 August 1908, a train carrying livestock left Llanymynech, went under the canal bridge at Carreghofa, entered the spur to the Llanfyllin line, and derailed. The engine, number 31, and just newly built, went over onto its side, badly damaging the track. The enquiry concluded that the accident was caused by excessive speed (though the report from the Advertizer said the train was only going at 15 miles an hour), but as a precautionary measure the class of engine was banned from the line. As can be seen from the pictures, it gathered, as accidents do, many people from the village, including school-children, though on that summer's day they were probably on holiday. It's astonishing that the train was removed and the line repaired and reopened in less than twenty-four hours.

Railway engine overturns – Remarkable accident on the Cambrian railway
– Marple gentleman's special train

An unusual accident, happily unattended by serious consequences, happened on the Cambrian Railway at Llanymynech on Friday. A special train
had brought on Mr Frank Barlow of Woodville, Marple, Lancashire, and
of Ystwm Colwyn, Meifod (brother of Sir Emmott Barlow), and his family,

No 31 derailed, children and other villagers sitting on the bank while the engine is still
smoking, the breakdown crane in the right background

and in taking some points some short distance from the station it left the rails and fell completely over on its side, drawing the rest of the train off the metals with it. Happily, the driver and stoker were able to jump clear in time to escape with their lives. The metals were doubled up like paper, one being so twisted as to resemble a wheel, while the sleepers were split up into matchwood.

The accident happened just about two o'clock, on a single line rail at a point 200 yards distant from Llanymynech station [*in fact almost a mile*]. The train was composed of Great Central stock, the engine, which weighed over 80 tons, being one of the five recently supplied to the Cambrian company by Messrs Beyer, Peacock, and Co., of Manchester. Behind it was a horse box containing two valuable animals. Next came a brake coach with eleven servants in it, then the saloon in which Mr Barlow and his family were travelling. Following this was another box with two horses, and in the rear was a brake van in which was Inspector Warwick, who was in charge of the train; and afterwards two covered carriage trucks.

The engine seems to have fallen foul of some points and turned on to a ballast siding, leaving the rails and taking the rest of the train with it. It ran over sleepers, breaking them up, as we have already stated, into matchwood as it went along, for a distance of 20 yards before the engine turned over on its right. One of its buffers partially telescoped the first horse van, but beyond this no other perceptible damage was done.

It was fortunate that the train was travelling at a very moderate speed, estimated at 15 miles an hour, otherwise the consequences would have been disastrous. As it was, the passengers escaped with only a severe shaking, Mr Barlow's eldest daughter, who received some bruises, being the only one to suffer injury.

What surprises the officials most is the wonderful escape of the driver and his stoker, and here it may be noted that the driver happened to be fireman on the old excursion train which met with such a terrible disaster at Welshampton eleven years ago, when 13 lives [*actually 11*] were lost.

Mr Denniss, general manager, with Mr Herbert Jones, locomotive superintendent, and Mr Macdonald, engineer, were soon on the spot, directing operations. A breakdown gang arrived about three o'clock from Oswestry, and the traffic for the remainder of the afternoon was held up on both sides, passengers on the Llanfyllin branch having to leave one train and take to another on arriving at the scene of the accident. By eight o'clock the line was reported clear once more, traffic being resumed in the morning after the line of metals had been repaired.

The cause of the accident is at present a mystery.

But forever after, only lightweight engines were allowed on the Llanfyllin branch.

44

The low cabin
LLANYMYNECH SIGNAL BOX

Llanymynech signal box, built in 1895, was made low so the signalman could see under the road bridge of the B4398. The operating floor was 8 feet 2 inches above rail level, and the box measured 26 feet by 9 feet.

ABOVE *The signal box from the south, inspected by an SLS rail tour around 1958. The box was 24 miles and 21 chains from Whitchurch Cambrian Junction signal box*
BELOW *The box from the north, in the early 1960s, with signalman Ern Beddow handing over the token for a Llanfyllin-bound passenger train*

ABOVE & LEFT
The box housed a Dutton type 3 frame with 47 levers. When the GWR took over, the box operated from 2.00am to 11.40pm or until the last train departed on Sunday. The token machines are top right, one for Llanymynech to Four Crosses, the other Llanymynech to Pool Quay, when Four Crosses box was closed. On the left in the middle is the tablet machine for Llanymynech to Llansanffraid (Ian Scrimgeour)

The paparazzi in Pant

DOLLY AND TOM JONES — THE PANT HEIRESS AND THE RAILWAY PORTER

The story of an 18 year old girl, Dolly Hopton, from a wealthy family, who eloped with the Cambrian Railways porter Tom Jones, made Pant famous throughout the country. It was the kind of story that made celebrities, briefly, of the couple, especially the girl, when she went on to use her fame to go on the stage at Oswestry. She seems to have lost her inheritance, but the marriage, though unfortunately short, did seem to be a happy one.

Evelyn Dorothy Hopton, a "jolly and bright eyed" eighteen-year-old girl, had been living with her mother at the Cottage, Pant. Her father worked in Uganda for the government, but when he left his post settled in the country to shoot big game. He wanted his daughter Dorothy, commonly known as Dolly, to follow the Protestant faith, because her mother was a Catholic. So Dolly was made a ward in chancery, with her mother having custody of her (though the expression 'ward in chancery' was often used when the child was illegitimate, which might explain Dolly's father's absence). The girl, however, used to attend services at Oswestry and Welshpool Catholic churches and two years previously was sent to a Catholic convent at Brussels. Apparently she didn't like the seclusion of the convent, and left after only eight weeks. Near the time of her elopement she claimed that some family friends were making arrangements for her to go to another convent. This seemed to have had some effect on her decision.

Tom Jones, the son of Mr Thomas Jones, a house decorator of Vron Vedw in Pant, was just nineteen. He had been educated at Llanymynech CE School, and worked for the Cambrian Railways for nearly 3 years, starting as a porter at Llanymynech station. He was employed at Llynclys railway station, at the small goods yard around where the Cambrian Heritage Railways have their sidings at present. Dolly and Tom had known each other for about nine months, though they had only been courting for five months. It seemed that everyone knew that they were "keeping company" except for Mrs Hopton. They decided to get married, but since they were both too young they needed the consent of their parents. Tom went to his father and asked him if he could get married, and his father apparently said, "Yes, you can get married twice over if you like," not thinking that Tom meant it. Dolly went to her mother in the same way, telling her she was thinking of getting married and asking her if it was all right, and Mrs Hopton, similarly not taking the girl at all seriously, said, "Yes, marry anyone who will have you."

So the couple decided to get married and went separately to Archdeacon Wynne Jones at Overly Hall, Oswestry, and he decided that everything was fine and allowed their request for a special licence. Tom went to Morton vicarage with the license and arranged with the vicar, the Rev CR Garnett Botfield, for the marriage the following day at one o'clock. The next morning he went to work as usual, spending the morning in the goods warehouse until lunchtime. He went to the signal box, took off his uniform, and put on the wedding suit he had left there. With his friend Hennery Lewis he walked across the fields to the church at Morton, telling his fellow employees he was going to look for birds. Meanwhile, Dolly had left her home telling her mother she was going to get half a dozen eggs. She called at Tom's home and persuaded his sister to accompany her on a walk. As soon as they were out of the house she told Tom's sister about the marriage plan, and his sister agreed to be a witness. They met Tom at the church, and the vicar married the couple. Afterwards, they walked to the station railway bridge, Tom kissed Dolly, and he went back to work.

Dolly went to her home, but someone had let the secret out, and before she arrived home she met a crowd, excited at the news. When she did get home she told her mother about the marriage. Mrs Hopton didn't believe her, thinking this was a joke, until she saw the wedding ring. Immediately Mrs Hopton telegraphed her solicitors in Liverpool, and sent a messenger to Welshpool so the priest, Father Moore, could come to the house. The girl was sent to her room to wait for the priest. When he arrived, Dolly let him in, but he immediately went to have a talk with her mother. Dolly decided to escape, and when the priest came out with Mrs Hopton to speak to Dolly, Dolly had left to meet Tom at the apartments they'd taken a mile away. Tom had been told off by his parents, but they had accepted what had happened and gave their blessings on the young couple. Father Moore and the family solicitors interviewed Tom the following Friday. Apparently Tom didn't know that his wife was a ward in chancery until the solicitor told him. The solicitor threatened him with two years prison but Tom didn't back down. They were married legally, he said, and there was no changing that. He and Dolly were living in furnished rooms at Pant, and had both talked to the Archdeacon, who asserted the legality of their marriage. Tom had also had an interview with Mrs Hopton. She suggested (we can imagine how strongly) that he should let Dolly return to her while he went away until he was 21. He refused, because, he said, he didn't know what would happen to his wife in the meantime.

A reporter from the Advertizer went about a week after the marriage to see the couple at Tom's parents' house. On the table there was a plate with some cake crumbs, the last of the wedding cake. Dolly "made merry over the whole affair". Both said they didn't want any enmity with any of their parents, but what they had done could not be undone. They were quite happy. They didn't know what turn events would take, but they thought the sooner the inevitable was accepted, the better.

OPPOSITE *A publicity photo for Dolly Jones' career on the stage, Tom in his Cambrian Railways porter uniform*

A reporter also went to see Mrs Hopton. She was not so cheerful, apparently thoroughly distressed over the marriage. The girl, she said, belonged to some of the best county families in England. "I did not know she knew the fellow," she remarked contemptuously. Asked if she had given her consent to the marriage, Mrs Hopton said, "I decline to discuss the matter with you." Asked about the convent in Brussels Dolly had been sent to, Mrs Hopton said that Dolly entered it by her own wish, to learn the language. "I took her there myself, and I thought she would be happy there. She did not like it, however, and left after being there a month." Mrs Hopton added that there had been no suggestion of sending Dolly back. She said that Dolly had been 'out', and had been attending balls and other social functions. Asked what her daughter's expectations were now, Mrs Hopton replied, "Absolutely nothing." She also added that as her daughter was a ward in chancery her consent to the marriage should have been obtained.

Two weeks later, the Advertizer reported that

Mrs Eveline [sic] Dorothy Jones, the heroine of the Pant romance, will make her first appearance on the stage at the British Animated Picture and Vaudeville Company's entertainment, of which Mr Davin Power is manager, attracted a crowded audience to the Public Hall, Oswestry, on Monday evening. A most entertaining programme was provided, and the artists included Miss Ethel Colier, a talented comedienne and dancer, and Lieutenant Harper, who was in his best form as a conjuror. The programme also included an excellent series of pictures, but the principal attraction was Mrs Jones, who was briefly introduced by Mr Power. Mrs Jones, who appeared in the uniform of a railway porter, had a most hearty welcome, and her singing of the song, "If you should have a tiny seed of love," evoked a well-deserved encore, in response to which she sang, "Have you got another girl like Mary." She was again enthusiastically recalled, and repeated her last song with much success.

In the course of a short interview our representative was informed by Mrs Jones that she had been the recipient of a large number of wedding presents, some of which were sent by unknown friends. She had also received numerous congratulatory messages. Asked whether it was true that she had been engaged by entertaining companies, Mrs Jones said that she had been communicated with through Mr Power, but she had refused to accept the offers of London and Manchester entertaining companies.

Despite her mother's disapproval the marriage seemed to be happy, and the couple had two sons. But on May 8, 1929, the Advertizer reported the death of Tom Jones:

Village romance recalled

The Late Mr Tom Jones, Pant

The passing away of Mr Thomas Edward (Tom) Jones, at the comparatively early age of thirty-eight, at his home, Vron Vedw, Pant, on Monday, May 6th, recalls memories of a twenty-year-old romance, when the little village of Pant suddenly became the rallying ground of pressmen from all parts of the kingdom. They were seeking information, snapping up every tiny detail surrounding the lives of Mr Tom Jones, then nineteen years old, and Miss Evelyn Dorothy Hopton, who became "the Pant heiress", and whose secret marriage, in romantic circumstances, to the youthful railway porter, became the leading "feature" in the news of the day. Death has now snapped the chain, but it is pleasing to record that, unlike many similar adventures, the "great experiment" turned out a success, and the married lives of Mr and Mrs Tom Jones has been most happy.

More information about Tom and Dolly was given in the obituary:

Born at Pant, at Canal Cottage, the late Mr Tom Jones was educated at Llanymynech CE School. He commenced his career as a porter at Llany-mynech station, in the old Cambrian regime, under Mr CE Williams, now stationmaster at Oswestry. Transferred to Oswestry North box, Mr Jones rose to the rank of first class signalman, a position he held for over twelve years. Married at Morton in 1909, he lived for a time at Breidden View, Pant, afterwards at Llwyn Road, Oswestry, later on taking up his perma-nent residence at Vron Vedw, where he lived up to the time of his death. The deceased has been a great sufferer from an internal complaint for the past seven years. In October, 1927, he was operated on at the Oswestry Cottage Hospital, and in February, 1928, underwent a second operation at St Thomas's Hospital, Westminster, London. It was at this hospital that Mrs Jones, who, throughout his long illness, had nursed her husband with untiring devotion, underwent the ordeal of blood transfusion, giving a pint and half of her blood when her husband lay in a most critical condi-tion. Mr Tom Jones returned to Pant apparently cured, but gradually the old trouble recurred and despite every attention, he passed away in the presence of his wife and mother on Monday week, leaving a widow and two sons to mourn their loss.

The funeral took place at Morton Parish Church on Thursday, and was attended by a large number of friends and sympathisers. Prior to the cortege leaving Vron Vedw, the Rev W Jones, Dolybran, Pant, conducted a short but impressive service. At the church the procession was met by the Rev HG Dickinson, rector of Llandysilio, who, in the absence of the Rev Garnett Bottfield, read the burial service. The hearse and coffin was cov-ered with wreaths, prominent among which was one sent by the GWR staff (Oswestry Station), composed of lilies and narcissi.

Following the death of her husband, Dolly Hopton raised her children alone and rented out rooms in her house to make extra money. She enjoyed paint-ing, especially on her visits to the small Cornish town of St. Ives.

Four Crosses and the Prince of Wales

The Llanfyllin branch became very busy in 1882, as the material for the dam at Lake Vyrnwy was transported through Llanymynech to Llanfyllin, and then by horse and cart to Llanwddyn. The dam was finished in 1888, and ten years later the diversions of the Cownwy and Marchnant streams were completed. On the 16th March 1910 HRH the Prince of Wales visited and commemorated the occasion by planting an oak tree. The Prince of Wales left his train at Four Crosses to go by car to the lake. The reason he didn't go by train all the way to Llanfyllin was almost certainly because the locomotive was too heavy for the Llanfyllin branch (after the Wern Junction accident), and perhaps it was thought too undignified to have the Royal Train pulled by one of the lightweight engines.

The crowds greeting the Prince of Wales at Four Crosses

Cambrian mishap

It's rather surprising what can derail a truck of several tons, as in this report:
A goods train for Llanfyllin left Oswestry about 10.30, and when nearing Llynclys station at a fair rate of speed, a bundle of clothes got jolted out of the wagon in which it was being conveyed, onto the line below. It fouled one of the rails, and the iron wheels, finding cloth more difficult to cut through than wood, a truck mounted the bundle and failing to regain the metals dropped into the six-foot way. The brakesman applied his brakes, and the engine driver was soon able to bring his train to a standstill. Both roads were fouled, and the services of a breakdown gang from Oswestry had to be requisitioned to restore the derailed wagon and clear the lines.
From the Advertizer, September 27, 1911

The Colonel's revival

THE SHROPSHIRE & MONTGOMERYSHIRE RAILWAY

The railway line from Shrewsbury to Llanymynech was reopened in August 1911, against all the odds, and most of the credit can go to one man: Holman Fred Stephens. He was always known as Colonel Stephens, though he was only a Lieutenant Colonel briefly in the First World War. He was a pioneer of light railways, having opened the Kent and East Sussex Light Railway at Tenterden. Light railways (like the Tanat Valley Railway between Llynclys and Llangynog) were a means of allowing railways that might not otherwise be built, not requiring specific legislation and allowing councils to contribute money. There was a weight restriction of 12 tons on each axle and speeds were a maximum of 25 miles an hour. Level crossings needed to be protected only by cattle grids and not gates.

The Shropshire Railways had been trying to resuscitate the old Potts line for almost two decades. In 1904, when the Tanat Valley Light Railway was suggested, the Shropshire Railways tried to get it to use their Nantmawr branch so the line would go into Llanymynech, but this came to nothing. Stephens negotiated with the directors of the Shropshire Railways in 1907, came to an

Richard Reeves, standing on the left on the trolley, was the only person employed to inspect the derelict Potts line, though on this 1903 trip he is accompanied by GM Perkins, standing next to him, Frank Fox-Davies, sitting on the left, TR Perkins, and Mr Morton. Fox-Davies took the photo, as he did many photos of Llanymynech and the area. He had a shop on the main street in Llanymynech (F Fox-Davies)

The five photos on these pages show the state of the Potts railway around the turn of the 19th century (all F Fox-Davies)

ABOVE *The original Potts station building at Llanymynech, with the fence dividing the Potts area and the Cambrian on the right. A fading 'Llanymynech' can just be made out on the top board*

BELOW *The track bed near Llanymynech. The old line is somewhere under the grass. This was what had to be restored*

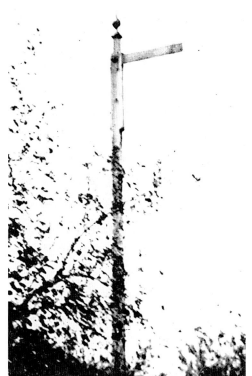

ABOVE LEFT *A close up of the McKenzie & Holland slotted signal from the Potts Railway, that can be just seen in the bottom left photo, opposite page*
ABOVE RIGHT *The Potts water tower, with a timber framework. A locomotive on the Cambrian side of the station accidentally burnt it down*
BELOW *The abandoned Potts locomotive shed at Llanymynech*

agreement, but suggested a new name: the Shropshire and Montgomeryshire Light Railway. The Montgomeryshire part was an 'appeal to local sentiment', especially as Montgomeryshire County Council supported the proposed company. The order for the new company was granted in 1909, signed by no less a person than Winston Churchill, though only because he happened to be President of the Board of Trade at the time.

Legal matters delayed the start of the rebuilding of the line until late in 1910, but as contractor, Stephens pushed on with the work, starting from the Llanymynech end, because that was in slightly better condition. Most of the sleepers – some 36,000 – were replaced, and the bridges repaired and locomotives bought, most notably the tiny Gazelle, said to be the smallest standard gauge locomotive ever built. The line was inspected in April 1911, and some more work carried out, ready for the grand opening.

Shrewsbury to Llanymynech. A run over the new line. Ready for opening. The journey by train direct from Shrewsbury to Llanymynech is reminiscent of a past generation. For thirty years the line which links up these two stations has lain derelict, grown over with briar and bramble, and in

The opening day of the Shropshire & Montgomeryshire Railway, when the train reached Llanymynech. In the right foreground are TR Perkins and FE Fox-Davies, who did so much to keep a record of the Potts Railway

THE RE-OPENED RAILWAY.

VIEWS ON THE SHREWSBURY AND LLANYMYNECH LINE.

"Advertiser" Photo.

1. View of Kinnerley Station, where are the headquarters of the new line.
2. Shrawardine Bridge over the Severn. The supports and girders were used by the old "Potteries" railway, but they have been thoroughly overhauled, and all the woodwork on the bridge is new.
3. A party of pioneers travelling over the line

before re-opening. Mr. Stephens, to whose enterprise and zeal the successful re-construction of the line is largely due, is leaning over the rail of the goods van. The inset is Mr. Reeves, who was guard of the last train which ran on the old line, and his seen been employed by the Official Receiver of the old company to look after what remained on the derelict line.

"Advertiser" I note.

parts buried in thick brushwood and copse. People had long shaken their heads in despair at the thought of ever seeing the Old Potteries as it was called re-opened, and its bad luck in the past had driven all faith in the venture out of the financiers. But its time has come and the permanent way, like a giant Rip Van Winkle, with arms stretching from the Severn at Shrawardine away into Shrewsbury and to Llanymynech, has had a great awakening. By the courtesy of the Managing Director, Mr HF Stephens, a couple of the members of the Advertiser staff last week had the pleasure of accompanying Mr Stephens on a trip over the line. The run over the line to Llanymynech takes the traveller through an exceedingly picturesque piece of country. To most people this country, owing to the lack of railway facilities in the past, is quite unknown, but in the days of the old Potteries Railway, no trips out of Shrewsbury were more popular than those that took pleasure seekers out into the pretty district around Red Hill or to that charming country around Ford or to that which abuts on the banks of the Severn at Shrawardine, while Nesscliff for its Hill, and on to Llanymynech, were resorts which were much in favour.
From the Oswestry and Border Counties Advertizer, April 12, 1911

LEFT *The report of the opening, from the Advertizer of April, 1911. Colonel Stephens is the man with the flat cap, leaning on the footplate*

The Reopened Railway.

Views on the Shrewsbury and Llanymynech line.

The Shropshire and Montgomeryshire railway was formally opened by the Mayor of Shrewsbury, Major Wingfield, on Thursday, when some two hundred gentlemen, members of public bodies which have subscribed to the undertaking, were invited, through the Deputy Mayor of Shrews-bury (Councillor Benjamin Blower) and the Managing Director (Mr HF Stephens) to join in a run over the line. The morning was gloriously fine, the first really warm day of spring, and in the bright sunshine the ani-mated scene at the Shrewsbury terminus of the new line, together with all the picturesque scenes along the route, made the restarting of the old railway an event to be remembered as accompanied by the pleasantest auspices and with a good augury for its future financial success.

The interest in the re-awakening of the railway to the traffic and the rattle of trains of the twentieth century, after its long sleep from far back in the nineteenth century, was shared to the full by folks all along the route and not the least of that interest was shown at the Llanymynech end, and on the arrival of the train at Llanymynech itself. Passengers generally were charmed with the beautiful scenery hereabouts; in fact, the beauty of the country from end to end of the line, and not the least the Llanymynech and Pant district were a pleasant surprise to a host of the travellers who were being taken through it for the first time.

The repaired and decorated S&M station building at Llanymynech

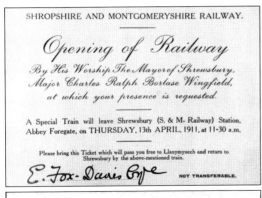

SHROPSHIRE AND MONTGOMERYSHIRE RAILWAY.

Opening of Railway

*By His Worship The Mayor of Shrewsbury,
Major Charles Ralph Borlase Wingfield,
at which your presence is requested.*

A Special Train will leave Shrewsbury (S. & M. Railway) Station,
Abbey Foregate, on THURSDAY, 13th APRIL, 1911, at 11-30 a.m.

Please bring this Ticket which will pass you free to Llanymynech and return to
Shrewsbury by the above-mentioned train.

E. Fox-Davies   NOT TRANSFERABLE.

CAMBRIAN RAILWAYS' ANNOUNCEMENTS.

NEW PLEASURE GROUNDS.

IDEAL SPOTS FOR PIC-NIC and SUNDAY SCHOOL PARTIES.

ON THURSDAY NEXT, and every succeeding Thursday
until further notice,
HALF-DAY TICKETS will be issued from OSWESTRY
by 2-42 p.m. train to

Maesbrook, Kinnerley, Nesscliff, and Shrawardine.

3rd return fares and times of return as under :—

	MAESBROOK.	KINNERLEY.	NESSCLIFF.	SHRAWARDINE.
Fare...	9d.	1/-	1/3.	1/6.
	p.m.	p.m.	p.m.	p.m.
Times of } From	5 7	5 0	4 54	4 48
Return. }	7 34	7 30	7 25	7 21

Oswestry arrive 7-13 and 8-0 p.m.

Shropshire & Montgomeryshire Railway.

SUPPORT THE LOCAL LINE.

THIS Line runs through a delightful country
and affords the travelling public every
possible facility for pleasure and trading.
There are numerous sites adjacent to the railway
system suitable for the erection of works and
factories of every description.

A Service of
RAIL MOTOR CARS
is now running between
**SHREWSBURY, FORD, LLANYMYNECH &
KINNERLEY.**

CHEAP EXCURSIONS
are run from Shrewsbury to Llanymynech for
GOLF LINKS,
and Fishing in the River Vyrnwy thereon and to
Criggion for the
BRIEDDEN HILLS.

CHEAP DAY EXCURSIONS
TO
CRIGGION AND LLANYMYNECH.

Five large Camping Huts adjoining the River
Severn, near Crew Green Station, have been
provided, and Rowing Boats are to be hired at
cheap rates.
The attractions are—Fishing, Rowing, Boating,
and Bathing. Sketching and Hill Climbing,
only half a mile from the Briedden Hills.
Camping Huts, 7/- per week per hut, and Weekly
Season Tickets, Third Class, to Salop at low rates.
10/- deposit on key of hut. Apply to Mr. John
Turner, District Traffic Agent, S. & M.R., Crewe
Green, Ford, or to J. L. White, Abbey Station.
H. F. STEPHENS, *Managing Director.*

SUPPORT THE LOCAL LINE.

The train ran into Llanymynech to the accompaniment of fog signals and cheers from the crowd gathered on the bridge. Unfortunately, the fact of the coming arrival of the train was little-known. Mr Kemble, the chairman of the Llanymynech Parish Council, was however on the platform, and he handed the following greeting to the Mayor of Shrewsbury and to the Managing Director: – "Llanymynech Parish Council. To Major Wingfield, Mayor of Shrewsbury, and HF Stephens, Esq, managing director Shropshire and Montgomeryshire Railway. Gentlemen, – Shortness of notice of the official opening of the Shropshire and Montgomeryshire Railway prevented arrangements being made by our Council to give you the official reception the occasion merits. I, therefore, as Chairman, extend to you on their behalf a most hearty welcome to our romantic village, and give expression to the general satisfaction the opening of the line affords. We congratulate those concerned on the speedy and thorough manner in which

TOP *The invitation to the opening of the S&MLR, for Frank Fox-Davies*

MIDDLE *Apparently supporting the S&M is this advert from the Cambrian Railways, featuring trips from Oswestry and along the S&M line for picnics*

BOTTOM *A advertisement for the S&M*

An ex-LNWR locomotive at Llanymynech. The carriage behind the tender used to be a royal coach

the work has been carried through. We appreciate the employment of so much local labour, and sincerely hope that the undertaking will be a financial success and an increasing benefit to the entire district. – Your obedient servant, John Kemble."

A stop of half an hour was made at Llanymynech, and the company in the interval had an abundant supply of sandwiches brought by the Deputy Mayor while the loving cup went round. The Deputy Mayor, in taking first the historic cup, raised it aloft and, amid cheers, drank success to the new line, and said with what pleasure they saw it open again and beginning its career under auspices so favourable. The return trip was made without a hitch, and Shrewsbury was reached by 3.30, after a very pleasant run.

The line was opened for public traffic on Good Friday. The weather was gloriously fine, and long before the hour – 1.45 p.m. – of the departure of the outgoing train from Shrewsbury passengers began to arrive in large numbers. By 1.30 an enormous crowd had collected, and those booking formed a long queue to the office. The most favoured stations were Llanymynech and Red Hill. Pretty well 250 booked, and the train steamed out amid cheers, which were kept up from the houses right through to Shrewsbury West and Meole Brace.

From the Oswestry and Border Counties Advertizer, April 19, 1911

But despite the 'auspices so favourable', this happened, in the first week of the S&MR's opening:

Mishap on the S. & M. railway

An unfortunate but happily not a serious mishap occurred to the 6 p.m.

train from Llanymynech, on Saturday. There were some forty passengers on the train, which consisted of the engine "Hesperus" and three coaches. The engine was running tender first, and, when approaching Red Hill station, the engine left the rails. The tender did not follow suit, but three of the five coaches came off. Happily, the speed at the time was only six or seven miles an hour, and beyond getting a good shaking no one, we are glad to say, was hurt.

The worst trouble was the inconvenience caused to the traffic. Sleepers and rails were knocked about, and the getting away of the derailed train and the repair of the permanent way occupied a breakdown gang until well on in the next day. In the meantime a large number of passengers were waiting at Abbey Foregate station to return to Llanymynech and elsewhere by the evening train. The track being a single line was, of course, quite blocked, and these passengers had to be despatched in motorcars and horse-drawn vehicles.

Mr Stephens, the managing director, was soon on the scene of the mishap, and took in hand the direction of operations. The incident, though only a trifling one, was unfortunate, happening as it did on the line with a single road, and general sympathy has been expressed for Mr Stephens in this

The carriage built for the London & South-Western Railway's royal train in 1848. It was bought by the S&M around 1926. Apparently it was abused by local children who either didn't know or didn't care about its origins, when they travelled to school in Shrewsbury. This photo was taken in 1935 at Llanymynech when it was used for an excursion (HF Wheeler)

little temporary setback to a concern which had made so auspicious a start, and on the satisfactory and thorough working of which the managing director on the day of the opening run was congratulated all round.

The line was cleared for traffic by Sunday afternoon, valuable assistance being given by London and North Western Railway breakdown gang. On Monday, over five hundred were conveyed in and out of Shrewsbury station.

From the Oswestry and Border Counties Advertizer, April 19, 1911

Llanymynech

Visitors. – The popularity of Llanymynech as a holiday resort appears to be increasing, and the Cambrian and Shropshire & Montgomeryshire Railways brought some hundreds into the district during the weekend. The hotels and apartment houses are nearly filled, and on Bank Holiday there was a large number of picnickers on the hill.

From the Oswestry and Border Counties Advertizer, October 11, 1911

On July 29, 1915, there was another derailment, on Shrawardine bridge, of the 2.30 p.m. out of Shrewsbury. It was said that 0-6-2T Thisbe broke a pony truck spring, but it may have been the fault of the bridge. The Manchester Guardian reported, "The bridge is 60 feet above the river, and if the passengers had got out of the coaches there was the possibility of falling through

0-6-0 No 3 Hesperus, one of the S&M's most famous engines, at Llanymynech. It was one of the S&MR's three LSWR Ilfracombe goods locomotives. Behind the tender is the saw mill, later a clog factory

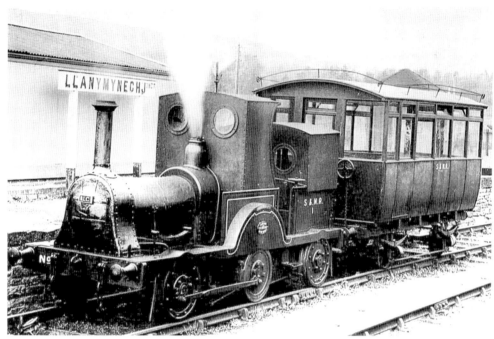

ABOVE *0-4-2WT No 1 Gazelle was the S&MR's most famous locomotive, perhaps mainly because it looks like a toy engine. It was built by Dodman at Kings Lynn in 1893, and brought to Shropshire in February, 1911. It was abandoned and restored several times, but was entirely suited to the S&M as an inspection vehicle, as it only weighed six tons. Withdrawn in 1950, but still preserved, it was said to be the smallest standard gauge locomotive built in this country. This photo was taken on April 23, 1939, on a Birmingham Locomotive Club rail tour. Note the sign on the platform is for Llanymynech Junction. The sign on the platform opposite claimed it was the 'Shortest Route to Shrewsbury' – it was, but unfortunately it wasn't the fastest*

BELOW *The S&M goods yard at Llanymynech, looking towards Maesbrook and Shrewsbury*

the white spaces between the girders. The women passengers were naturally greatly alarmed. One fainted in the coach, while another fell out onto one of the girders. A Shrewsbury solicitor, Mr EP Lewis, who was travelling on the train, clutched her on the girder and saved her from falling through into the river. It was nearly an hour before she could be persuaded to release her hold and was carried off the bridge."

Though the railway seemed to start well, despite the derailment in its first week, it was never financially viable. Not that it made huge losses, but it always owed money. The traffic from Criggion Quarry helped, and if the S&MR could have regained the traffic from the Nantmawr quarries it might have been a success. But the Cambrian Railways, not surprisingly, didn't help the Shropshire & Montgomeryshire in any way, and managed to obstruct Stephens when he attempted to get back use of the Nantmawr branch, which the Cambrian Railways had leased in 1900 for 99 years (though there had been an earlier proviso that the Shropshire Railways could use it on six months' notice). During 1920, in particular, Stephens wrote constantly to the Cambrian's General Manager to try and get some agreement, all without success.

Stephens became ill in 1930, and died in 1931. Only then was it discovered how dire was the financial state of the Shropshire & Montgomeryshire. The debt it owed to the bank was very slowly reduced, and some improvements were made to the track, but passenger numbers continued to fall. In 1933, with passenger numbers down to just over 3000 a year, it was decided to suspend the passenger service. Special trains were occasionally run, but by 1939 the company was in a terrible state. It was saved by the Second World War.

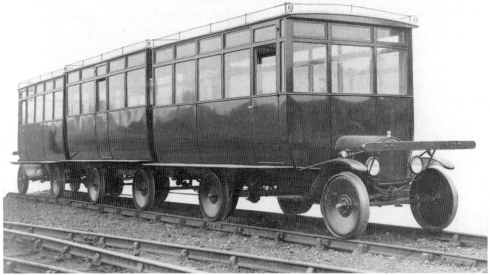

The three car Ford passenger railmotor, noisy, slow and shaky. It was bought in 1923 to reduce costs, but sold for scrap in 1943

God's Wonderful Railway
THE GREAT WESTERN RAILWAY

The Great Western Railway was rather hated by Cambrian Railways employees and directors – no 'God's Wonderful Railway', as the GWR liked to call themselves, for the Cambrian – because the GWR always opposed almost everything the Cambrian Railways did, almost as a matter of principle. But in 1920 the government decided that the railways were in such a terrible state (mainly because the government hadn't paid the compensation they'd promised during the First World War) that the structure of 178 independent companies had to be reformed. There were to be four companies, and the western one would be the GWR, and it would take over almost all the Welsh companies, including the Cambrian Railways, the largest of the Welsh companies.

On 25 March 1922 the Cambrian Railways was amalgamated with the GWR. This was an elegy written for the Advertizer that week, by someone calling himself a Philosopher of the Prowl:

By the way: the Passing of the Cambrian.

I wonder how many people who travelled on the Cambrian on Saturday realised they were attending a funeral. Well, not quite a funeral, perhaps; at any rate not a funeral of the ordinary sort, for, on Monday morning the corpse was, to all outward appearances as lively as ever, whistling its

A GWR 'Bulldog' in the 1930s at Llanymynech

In 1932, GWR No 849 with a down goods

way along the Severn Valley and over the Montgomeryshire mountains as if nothing outward as happened. But behind the scenes something very significant had occurred during the weekend. As we were putting on our clocks and pretending it was "summertime," the Cambrian, after its long and arduous struggle against adversity had officially ceased to be. Today it is a section – a fairly important section we may hope, even when seen through Paddington glasses – but still, just a section of the Great Western. As an independent Company its life is at an end.

And what a life of wrestle and romance it had been to be sure! Born, away back in the early fifties [*1850s, of course*], as a tiny baby, without arms or legs, and only just a small trunk – reaching from Newtown to Llanidloes, of all places on this mortal earth – its limbs developed gradually, one of them, from Newtown to Oswestry, only after some excruciating growing pains, under the agony of which it sometimes seemed as if this poor little child must succumb. But for the careful nursing of his parents, and "Drs" David Davies of Llandinam, and Thomas Savin of Oswestry, it probably would. And then how much poorer our local life in this part of the Welsh border would have been! What familiar names, long associated, not only with the railway itself but with the civic and philanthropic life of the district into which their official duties had brought them, would have been omitted from our role of public men of the past generation – Benjamin Piercy, George Owen, George Lewis, John Conacher, Thomas Savin himself, once the hero of a hundred fights in the Parliamentary committee rooms, and on the occasion of the final victory of the Oswestry, Ellesmere, and Whitchurch Railway, welcomed back on his return to Oswestry from London with the pomp and circumstance of an emperor. But what days those were, which our fathers still delight to tell, when battle after battle had to be waged at Westminster against the great "vested interests" of the giant companies who, in their fear and jealousy, would, if they could, crush the life out of their little "independent" rival! But they could not. Time and again the little "independent" company triumphed, and first one link in another was forged in the iron chain that ultimately bound Whitchurch and Aberystwyth, and Pwllheli, and became consolidated, in 1864, as "The Cambrian Railways".

And so the company struggled on to youth and maturity. Old engines with grandiloquent names, "Albion", "Prince of Wales", "Tubal Cain", "Mountaineer", "Prometheus", and the like, gave place to new, if un-christened monsters, small rattling old coaches on four iron wheels developed into long bogey corridor carriages in which one can not only travel in comfort, but wash, eat and drink – at any rate tea. Wooden bridges disappeared to make room for iron and steel girders and the magnificent station-masters of the sixties, with their top hats and their sixteen shillings a week to

A 1937 photo of the GWR tracks on the left and the S&M tracks on the right, 'Llanymynech Junction' on the S&M side. No 5816 is about to push the branch train to the yard (RK Cope)

enable them to support the dignity, bowed themselves out and vacated platforms now commanded by businesslike agents of more modern if less impressive sartorial adornments.

More than sixty years in some parts of the system, can the memory of its veteran servants go back to the time, when, as an aged ex-driver, now living happily on his pension in a Montgomeryshire town, told me the other day, "Things were very comfortable then, very comfortable." "Things", in fact, did not seem to matter much at all in those days. Punctuality was not insisted upon, or even if it was, was not obtained. Trains could arrive an hour or so late and nobody appeared to worry much. The world was not in such a hurry, and "catching connections", about which the bustling passenger makes such a to-do today were a matter of luck rather than of scientific precision.

But the Cambrian has long ago sown this sort of wild oats. Today it is a highly respected member of the community of railways whose directors and officials can even afford to publish periodic statistics announcing the small proportion of trains which run behind time, and even when they do it is generally the fault of the "other boy" – the great lines that feed them at Whitchurch or Dolgelley or Afonwen. Anyhow, take it all in all, the Cambrian can look back upon its long life with equanimity. Obstacles and trials and tribulations have marked the years, as they do in the lives of most of us. There have been days of joy and days of sorrow. But it has had a useful if strenuous career and served its day and generation faithfully and well. And now the end of that life, as a separate existence, is come. The "poor old Cambrian", which we have known, and laughed at, and cursed, and loved, for all these years, officially, is no more. For the present, as I have already said, there may be little or no visible change to the public eye. The familiar black engines, drawing the equally familiar dark green coaches, will continue to pass along the old familiar track. But they will be serving a new master – a master who may at any time decide to reclothe them in his own livery, of green and chocolate, and write his well-known initials, "GWR", over all. Well, I suppose one can get used to such a change in time, and in years to come a new generation will arise to whom it will seem the obviously natural thing that Great Western engines should career through Ellesmere and Llanymynech and nose their way up to Llanfyllin and Llangynog. But amongst those who have watched the Cambrian grow middle-aged and old and die – at any rate officially – no one will drop upon its grave a sincere here than:

A Philosopher of the Prowl
From the Advertizer, March 1922

ABOVE *August 5,1935, 2388 with an up goods. There's a horse box in the bay siding – that area was used for horses for Llanymynech races. On the extreme right can be seen part of the weighbridge office. It's the only building from Cambrian days left on the site in 2012*

BELOW *On the same day, a schoolboy inspects Collett 0-4-2T No 5816 as it waits with an Oswestry to Llanfyllin service. 'Llanfyllin, Llanymynech, and Oswestry' is written on the carriage (HF Wheeler)*

The Cambrian always insisted that they took over the GWR and not the other way round, but, whichever, it was an arrangement that was needed. The Cambrian Railways had never made much money, and might have had to close many of its branch lines if it hadn't been for the grouping with the GWR. Changes were few and small. The GWR station at Oswestry was closed, so passengers didn't have to walk between the two stations. The freight service from Llanymynech to Blodwel junction was withdrawn, in 1925.

ABOVE *On the same day as the previous two photos, Bank holiday Saturday afternoon, ex-Cambrian 0-6-0 No 893 on a train for Welshpool*

LEFT *A GWR poster for the horse races at Llanymynech, on May 10, 1930*

OPPOSITE BELOW *Taken on the same day as opposite above, this is from beneath the road bridge. The GWR train is different to the one opposite above, 4812 with the 11.13 Llanymynech-Llanfyllin (W A Camwell, Stephenson Locomotive Society Library Collection 2575)*

ABOVE *Engines on both sides of the station, from the road bridge: nearest the camera War Department 70084 (originally Great Eastern), and on the GWR down platform 90xx. Taken on August 26, 1946 by W A Camwell (Stephenson Locomotive Society Library Collection 2576 1946 90xx + WD70084)*

ABOVE *Ex-Cambrian Railways 0-6-0 No 910 on the up goods at Llanymynech*

BELOW *Ex-Cambrian Railways 4-4-0 No 1043 arrives from Oswestry (SW Baker)*

Richard Roberts's station

CARREGHOFA HALT

Carreghofa council badgered the GWR for several years for a station. Carreghofa was the birthplace (probably at the tollhouse at Newbridge) of Richard Roberts, Llanymynech's most famous person. He was an inventor, and co-founder of Sharp, Roberts and Co, which, under its later name of Sharp, Stewart and Co, provided many locomotives for the Cambrian, including some of the very first. The GWR had a policy of opening halts, very small unstaffed stations, where trains stopped only by request. It opened Park Hall for the army camp and the orthopaedic hospital, and finally, on April 11 1938, the GWR opened a halt at Carreghofa. The halt was on the old Nant-mawr branch of the Potts railway, just before the bridge under the canal and the deviation to the Llanfyllin branch.

ABOVE *Carreghofa Halt on the day of opening, April 11, 1938, the shelter then unpainted timber. The large sign is now at the Cambrian Railways Museum in Oswestry*

BELOW *The small enamel sign (an enamel lamp tablet) from the halt*

ABOVE *An Ivatt Mogul 2-6-0 2MT (railway buffs refer to them affectionately as 'Mickey Mouse' engines) on a lush summer's day. Trains went tender first to Llanfyllin, as here, and engine first back to Llanymynech, as bottom right*

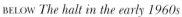

BELOW *The halt in the early 1960s*

ABOVE *Guard Tom Lunt on the platform with Ivatt 2MT 46512 and the Llanfyllin to Oswestry train in 1963*

BELOW *Ivatt 2-6-0 2MT 46512 again (P Ward)*

Bits & pieces
LLANYMYNECH STATION

ABOVE *Llanymynech Station in October 1958 (HC Casserley)*

BELOW *From under the road bridge, Llanymynech Hill behind, September 1962*

Opposite can be seen the wonderful mixture of buildings that was Llanymynech Station. From left to right: in the bits of buildings nearest the road bridge is first the lamp room (later the iron mink truck by the bay platform was used to keep the lamps and fuel, for safety reasons), the gents lavatory, the open waiting area with seats (this was probably the original Oswestry & Newtown station building), the Station Master's office; in the building with the canopy (possibly also Oswestry & Newtown), was the waiting room and ticket office, and the ladies waiting room; to the right and set back from the footbridge were the refreshments rooms, third class and first class (though I don't know what the difference between them was).

In the background at the top is the large white house now as Glan Verniew, or, now, Glan Vyrnwy. It was built before the railways came to Llanymynech, probably in 1771, as a coaching house.

RIGHT *These BR plans were for the track rationalisation when the S&M connection with the Down line was singled in February 1954. They show the layout of the station in some detail*

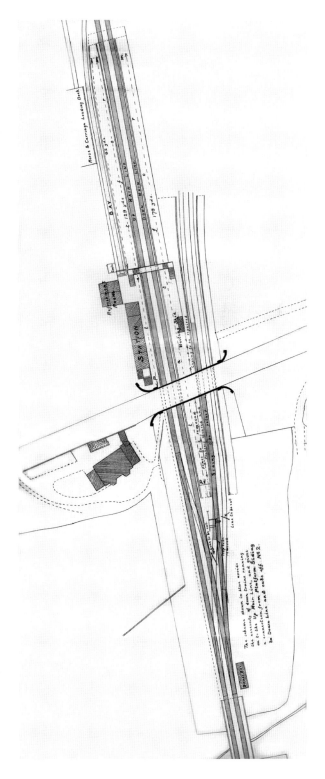

ABOVE *Most country stations were originally purely functional buildings. Later, most were rebuilt, so station staff could live there, and so that they would be more impressive objects. Four Crosses station was a good example of this, but Llanymynech remained almost as it was when first built, with odd buildings and sheds tacked on, as can be seen from this view of its roofs*

BELOW *It was said that no two Cambrian Railways footbridges were the same, and certainly the one at Llanymynech was unusual*

ABOVE *The refreshment rooms, used by local lads to avoid being seen in the village pubs. Nellie Beeston (see the photo on page 135) ran the rooms. The last licensee was FW Hughes & Sons of Welshpool, though before that Spiers & Pond had the licence, for most of the time*
BELOW *The rooms closed on September 29, 1957 (probably because of an ASLEF strike)*

ABOVE *The entrance to the station. The gate and the post with its metal protective post survive in 2012 (see page 124)*

BELOW *A closer view of the buildings, though in 1966, a year after closure. The way in to the ticket office was through the double doors on the right*

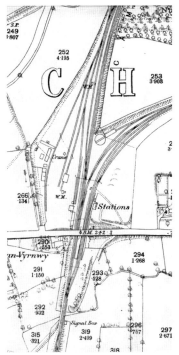

ABOVE LEFT *Looking north, towards the road bridge. To the right of the signal box is the remains of a Cambrian Railways coach body. The occasion is a rail tour, with the 0-6-0 tank engine on the S&M line*

ABOVE RIGHT *Llanymynech in 1887, showing the layout of the rails, including the Potts turntable to the right of the Cambrian main line*

BELOW *A drawing by the Cambrian Railways of the station and yard, from around the First World War. There is a fowl house, sawdust store, joiner's shop, and examiner's hut*

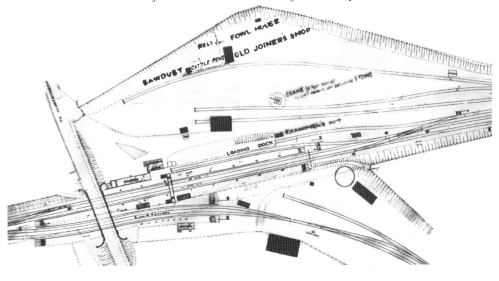

ABOVE *The goods shed (the far half built by the Cambrian), with piles of scrap metal around, was used to repair or take apart wagons and carriages – March 1963 (ME Lloyd)*

BELOW *The goods yard in the early 1960s, from near the entrance, the cattle siding (originally) on the left, the weighbridge office on the right*

ABOVE *Looking north. The bay signal, at least, is a Cambrian original. The ground frame, controlling the yard, was originally a signal box (PJ Garland Collection Per RS Carpenter)* BELOW *A view of some of the station sidings, carriages and wagons waiting repair or, in the 1960s, breaking up. The bay siding on the left was for coal and animal feed*

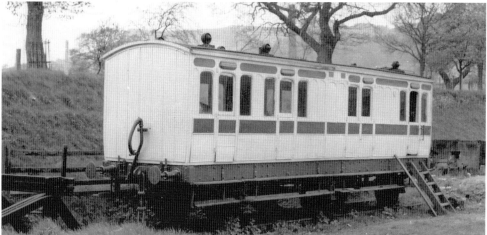

OPPOSITE, TOP *This was a Manchester, Sheffield & Lincolnshire Railway 4 wheeler coach that was brought to Llanymynech yard by Station Master John E Humphreys in the early 1930s for a man who worked at Llanymynech Station, whose house in Pant burnt down. This photo was taken not long after the coach had been installed*
OPPOSITE, MIDDLE *This was taken in April, 1954, when it looks newly painted*
OPPOSITE, BELOW *And this in September, 1958, when abandoned , to the right an auto train. The railings round the oak trees of Llanymynech playing fields can be seen in the background (HC Casserley)*

Wagon Repair

The Central Wagon Repair Company Depot moved from Oswestry to Llany-mynech in June 1946 and was provided with a yard which was situated on the west side of Llanymynech station, and it was here that wagons and some carriages were brought to be repaired or broken up. The work was mainly intended for forces people returning from the war, with up to 20 men working there at a time. Later the company changed to the North Wales Wagon Company. The old wagons for breaking up were mainly open ones with grease boxes. If there were too many to deal with they were put in the old branch bay behind the ground frame, with some even being stored on the old Potts line. Brian Rowe, fireman on the mainline, remembers that wagons were often simply set on fire to remove the wood.

All up freight trains passing from the up line into the yard would have been brought to a stand at the up main to yard signal and before any movement was made by the man operating the ground-frame he communicated by telephone with the signalman at Llanymynech south signal box.

LEFT *The only locomotive broken up at Llanymynech was this Churchward 2-8-0 No 2869. Jack Beeston and his great niece Jane & great nephew David stand by and on it in 1963 (Tony Beeston)*

An aerial photo of Llanymynech station, taken by the War Department in 1948. It shows the large number of trucks in the sidings, waiting for repair or to be taken apart. Rock Siding, going from the top right to middle left, is clearly disused, but the canal seems full of water. The long shadow of the Hoffmann kiln is visible, top left

Bobby Charlton at Llanymynech
THE SHROPSHIRE & MONTGOMERYSHIRE RAILWAY & THE WAR DEPARTMENT

When the war started in September 1939 it was realised that ammunition depots were needed. Several places were considered, but Shrawardine and Nesscliff were decided upon, mainly because there was a suitable railway nearby – the Shropshire and Montgomeryshire. An agreement was reached in 1940 so that the S&M could continue with its civilian traffic, especially the stone from Criggion quarry, while War Department personnel operated their trains.

Most military traffic went from the depots to Red Hill, at Shrewsbury, but Llanymynech to Kinnerley was kept for emergency, as Shrawardine viaduct was considered vulnerable to bombing. Llanymynech was busy, as there was a demand for Criggion stone to make runways for planes. The bridge at Melverley was replaced by the GWR in 1941, and when the branch was reopened the traffic went to Kinnerley, and then to Llanymynech and the main line between Oswestry and Welshpool. Gazelle was used on the line as the first train of the day to make sure there had been no damage during the night.

The Llanymynech end of the line was also used to carry army personnel as passengers, including to dances at Llanymynech and Pant, and perhaps for local football matches. In fact it's known that Bobby Charlton and Duncan Edwards (who was killed in the plane crash at Munich in 1958) were stationed at Nesscliff during their national service. There is a story that when Bobby Charlton came to Llanymynech to play for Nesscliff against the local team, John Edward Humphreys, then the Station Master at Llanymynech, was so impressed he tried to sign the lad – but unaccountably the young Bobby Charlton refused, preferring, apparently, to play for a team called Manchester United. The history of English football – and of Llanymynech – might have been very different if Mr Humphreys had been successful.

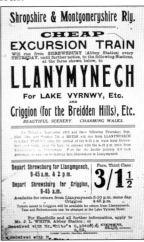

Staff at Llanymynech station

These were the Station Masters at Llanymynech from the Oswestry & New-town Railway through to British Railways:

1860 - 1862   Mr Saffrey
1862 - 18??   Mr Johnson (the Booking Clerk was Mr RR Roberts)
18?? - 1900   Mr E Wilson (transferred to Tylwch)
1900 - 1901   Mr J Jones (transferred to Pwllheli)
1901 - 1902   Mr T Bowen (left to become a canvasser)
1902 - 1904   Mr T Price (transferred to Three Cocks Junction)
1904 - 1908   Mr Charles Williams (transferred to Llanidloes; he won the
best kept station award while at Llanymynech)
1908 - 1922   Mr Ebenezer Davies (transferred to Barmouth)
1922 - 1930   Mr Arthur W Reed (retired)
1930 - 1954   Mr John Edward Humphreys (retired) [see *opposite page*]
1954 - 1961   Mr Edward Evans (retired)
1961 - 1965   Mr Heston Matthews (line closed)

Some Llanymynech staff: on the left a photo from the 1930s, with Bert Saunders, 'lad', on the left, and F Griffiths, the signalman, on the steps of the signal box. The photo on the right seems to show two Station Masters, judging by the caps, though it seems to be a last day joke on January 17, 1965, as the man on the left is Charlie Humphreys, the signalman

320 years of service

THE HUMPHREYS RAILWAY FAMILY

This appeared in the April 1954 County Times postbag:
Dear Sir – My brothers and I have been very interested in the paragraphs which appeared in "The County Times" on 20 March and 10 April regarding the railway service of two families.
I would point out that my family can easily beat either record; the highest so far recorded is 180 years, attained by the family of Mr Tom Leighton of Buttington, but our total is over 320 years and we could go much higher

if necessary by including husbands of grandchildren. However, we consider it quite sufficient to include only those on the attached list: my father (deceased); his six sons; one grandson; and a daughter-in-law. You will observe that the service of the sons alone is 231 years - and that we are all still working on the railway. I think that our record of railway service will take a lot of beating anywhere in the British Isles.
Yours faithfully,
J E Humphreys, Station Master, Llanymynech (left)

The late William Humphreys, of The High, Pant, Railway Ganger at Llynclys, retired in 1929 and died same year (50 years service)
All the following are still working [in 1954]:
John Edward Humphreys, Station Master at Llanymynech for over 23 years (45 years service)
William Henry Humphreys, employed at Pant for last 30 years (43)
Alfred Humphreys, Goods Guard at Oswestry (41)
Walter Humphreys, Goods Guard at Oswestry (39)
Charles Humphreys, Signalman at Llanymynech (29)
John Humphreys (grandson) a clerk in the District Traffic Superintendent's Office in Oswestry (11)
Mrs M Humphreys (Daughter-in-law), Crossing Keeper at Pant (30)
[omitted, possibly by the County Times, was Samuel Humphreys, who was a Guard at Oswestry; his son John did another 40 years plus on the railways]

The posher station
FOUR CROSSES STATION

ABOVE *Four Crosses station – rather grander than the one at Llanymynech, even after closure (Snowy Owen collection)*

BELOW *7812 Erlestoke Manor calls in at Four Crosses on the last week of services*

ABOVE *80135 BR Standard Tank 2-6-4 locomotive arriving at Four Crosses with the 8.17 am Oswestry-Aberystwyth train on Monday, May 27th, 1963 – the school train. The driver was Jack Holloway, of the Wern at Llanymynech (Colin Jenkins)*

BELOW *Staff at Four Crosses, from left to right: Porter Alf Roberts, Station Master Gwilym Williams, & Signalman Tom Parry*

ABOVE *7819 Hinton Manor calling at Four Crosses, on its way to Welshpool*

BELOW *The goods yard at Four Crosses. The coach body on the right was removed piece by piece by John Humphreys (Llanymynech Station Master John Edward Humphreys' son), and carried home on his bike to remake as a cold frame*

ABOVE *Standard tank engine 2-6-4T coming into Four Crosses from Llanymynech*

BELOW *In January 1965, almost the last day for Four Crosses*

No station master

PANT STATION

The first mention of Pant station comes just before the opening of the Oswestry and Newtown Railway, when it was called the Pant Crossing:
The Pant – on Mondays, first, second and third class return tickets, at a fare and a half for the double journey, will be issued at the Pant Crossing for Pool Quay, by the trains leaving Oswestry at 9.15 and 11.20 a.m.
Pant was not considered an important enough station to have a station master. Instead it had a Leading Porter, which for a while in the 1920s was one of the Humphreys family, William Henry, brother of Llanymynech Station Master John E Humphreys.

Mal Humphreys – not a member of the Humphreys railway family – lived in Pant in the 1960s, working at the wages office in the Cambrian locomotive works at Oswestry. He recalls that the engine would sound its whistle three times as it left Llanymynech, which told everyone they had to hurry down to Pant station to catch the train to work or school.

Hilton Holmes tells the story that his father, Albert Holmes, a driver on the Cambrian lines, told him, about a garden in Pant that had a scarecrow. The garden being close to the railway, the firemen on the engines always used to lob coal at the scarecrow, to try and knock it down. The canny owner of the garden used to leave the scarecrow there – so he never had to buy coal.

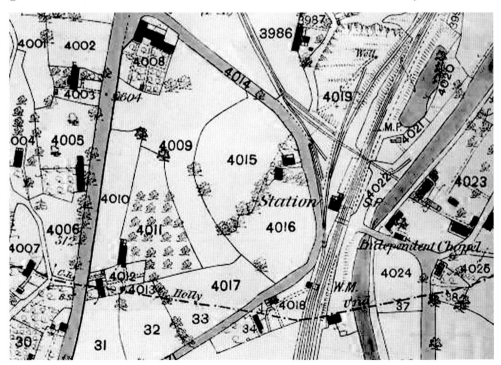

ABOVE *Pant signal box and station from the canal. This photo illustrates how close the canal and railway were. The smaller bridge was probably for a tramway, before the railway came to Pant*

LEFT AND BELOW *Pant Station from just above the canal (see page 128 to look at how it is now). There was a triangle taken out of the station house, on the left of the gates. Mike Robinson, who as a child lived there (in fact the boy in the colour picture on page 97), believes that this was because of the tramway, to fit the house into that piece of land. The 1890s map of the layout of Pant Station seems to bear this out, as it shows the profusion of tramways connecting to the railway and canal*

ABOVE *Leading porter William Henry Humphreys at Pant as a Llanfyllin bound train arrives*
BELOW *Two views of Pant signal box, on the east side of the station*

ABOVE *The crossing gates at Pant, unusually shut to the line, either after letting a car over, or possibly on a Sunday, when they could be left open all day (Willy Cossey)*

LEFT *A family gathering in the early 1960s at Pant signal box steps – though not all lived in the station house! Those who worked on the railways are: back, Sid Upson, signalman at Weston Rhyn, and Sam Robinson, BR Deputy Regional Fire Officer at Crewe; middle, Theresa Robinson (nee Humphreys), Crossing Keeper at Pant from her mother Madeleine's retirement to the closure of the line in 1965, Madeleine Humphreys, W.H. (Bill) Humphreys, Leading Porter at Pant (Willy Cossey)*

BR days
LLANYMYNECH & BRITISH RAILWAYS

ABOVE *On May 16, 1956, 9008 enters Llanymynech with a down passenger train*
BELOW *Also in 1956, pannier tank 0-6-0PT 7400 class 7410 arrives with a pick-up goods*

When the Great Western Railway was nationalised into British Railways on January 1, 1948, the effect on the railways around Llanymynech was small. The Tanat Valley line was closed from Blodwel Junction to Llangynog in December, 1960, though the line from Llynclys Junction to Nantmawr was kept open for quarry traffic. In 1963 the old Cambrian Railways lines were transferred from the Western Region to the London Midland Region, ruled in effect from Euston, the home of the old London & North Western Railway, even more hated by the Cambrian Railways than the GWR.

ABOVE *46506 arrives with the Llanfyllin to Oswestry train in May, 1956 (the late Geoff Bannister, courtesy Andrew Bannister)*
BELOW *In the early 1960s, 0-4-2 1458 has arrived with an up local passenger train*

ABOVE *4-6-0 Foxcote Manor leaves Pant for Llanymynech and Welshpool, taken by the canal. The barn still exists, as does Foxcote Manor, preserved and based on the Llangollen Railway*

BELOW *A view of Pant station, an Ivatt 2MT with an Oswestry train about to leave, taken from above the piggeries on September 9, 1964 (Joan Jones)*

ABOVE *On May 11, 1965, 46507 arrives at Llanymynech with a down local passenger train to Llanfyllin*

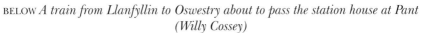

BELOW *A train from Llanfyllin to Oswestry about to pass the station house at Pant (Willy Cossey)*

A railway tragedy

THE DEATH OF LLEWELYN JONES

This was the report in the Advertizer on Wednesday, April 10, 1957, of a railwayman who was killed replacing the bridge at Llanymynech over the River Vyrnwy. He fell from the bridge, and must have knocked his head on a metal tube at a particularly deep part of the river, where the water swirled round the uprights. One of his mates managed to get hold of him and tried to pull him up, but was in danger of himself drowning and had to let go.

Another railway tragedy - Third in a month on Oswestry-Welshpool stretch of line - Workman's fall from bridge into river Vyrnwy

Three railwaymen have now lost their lives within a short space of a month on the Oswestry-Welshpool stretch of the line. On Sunday evening 50-year-old bridgeman Llewelyn Jones, married and with a family, fell from a girder on the northern side of the Llanymynech railway bridge into the river Vyrnwy and lost his life. Mr Jones came from Caersws. Efforts by four of his workmates failed to save him although Mr John Emrys Noel Davies, who became exhausted in the swift current and overcome by the cold, had to let him go to save his own life.

Jones disappeared and his body was not recovered until 9.30 a.m. on Monday, 20 yards below the bridge on the Montgomeryshire side of the

Looking east at the new bridge over the River Vyrnwy at Llanymynech, the Breidden Hills and Rodney's Pillar in the background

A photo taken for the Advertizer at the time of Llewelyn Jones' death. A Wickham trolley is by the signal

river. Davies was also in difficulties but managed to hang onto the lifebelt thrown into the river and was pulled from the water. The other three who dived to help Jones were Percy Smout and Walter Lloyd of Caersws, and Edward Meredith of Llandinam. Jones's body was carried down stream under the bridge in mid-river where the estimated depth of the water is 20 feet.

Work has been going on for the past week reconstructing the bridge and moving the line. A film was taken recently of the work for Transport Commission records and instructional purposes. A workman on the scene of the accident on Monday told the Advertizer that Jones appeared to put up little fight after hitting the water. "Everything had gone so well until then," he said.

A post-mortem was held on Monday at Welshpool.

On March 10 this year, a Sunday, a Caersws man who was a member of the permanent way gang working on a bridge at Pool Quay, less than 6 miles from the scene of Sunday's accident, was crushed to death whilst under the bridge. The same day a Shrewsbury man, the leading figure of the crane travelling to Pool Quay from Shrewsbury, was killed when the crane hit a footbridge at Buttington, near Welshpool, and demolished it.

ABOVE *7821 Ditcheat Manor approaches the bridge over the Vyrnwy with an Up passenger train from Four Crosses on January 14, 1965 (Neil Parkhouse collection)*

BELOW *46512 calls at Carreghofa Halt on September 1, 1964. The train delivered an important item for Carreghofa School (at the top left) – milk for the children*

Looking up at the underside of the bridge (for two tracks) under the canal and B4389 at the Wern, near Carreghofa School
ABOVE *The iron trough that carries the canal*
BELOW *The superb brick work by the Potts engineers – part of the grand push to Ireland*

The last branch
THE LLANFYLLIN LINE

A branch line that still lives
by Cynric Mytton-Davies
From the Advertizer, April 27, 1960

The Tanat Valley line is closed, so is the Shropshire and Montgomeryshire, the Llanfair Caereinion and the Kerry. The only branch line on the Cambrian system between Oswestry and Aberystwyth that remains open is the one to Llanfyllin. How is it that the Llanfyllin branch has remained open when all the rest are being closed down? Wondering about this while I was over in Llanfyllin I went along to the station to find out, and met the stationmaster, Mr Roderick Richards, and put the question to him.

You're not really aware of the part the railway plays in the life of Llanfyllin because the station is hidden behind the county library; you have to go down a side turning to reach it and then some way round the next corner at the far end of the approach yard. It's right at the very edge of the town, and consists of a single platform with the usual waiting rooms, booking hall and station house, and with sidings and the goods warehouse beyond. A bill pasted on a board near the entrance advertises cheap day tickets to Oswestry, Shrewsbury, Wrexham, Manchester and Liverpool, so obviously the line is well used.

Mr Richards reminded me that Llanfyllin is entirely dependent on the railway for its transportation. There is no regular daily bus service to Oswestry – or anywhere else. There are the local market services but nothing in the way of a standard fare stage system of buses. So people without cars use the train, and the branch continues to attract passenger traffic in consequence. Who are the people who use this line? There are between 12 and 20 commuters who work in Oswestry and go backwards and forwards on the business trains; about 80 or 90 schoolchildren in term time, and any number of Llanfyllin housewives for shopping in Oswestry. The commuters' and shoppers' traffic is outward, but the school traffic is inward, bringing children from Llanymynech, Llansantffraid and Llanfechain to school in the town.

Strangely enough nobody runs a season ticket; it wouldn't pay them. There's a special cheap return ticket from Llanfyllin to Oswestry which costs only 2s 5d, and this works out cheaper for six days' travelling and weekly season-ticket. The special cheap fare was introduced about five years ago to attract fresh traffic and enable the line to be kept open. It has evidently succeeded in its purpose. But where a dozen and a half people commute to Oswestry today, six years back there were nearer forty.

On the freight side, there's a steady traffic in animal feeding stuffs and fertilisers, and much of this is centred on the Wynnstay and Montgomery-shire Farmers' Association headquarters at Llansantffraid. But there's also a rather odd traffic in horses. I watched three lots of three horses that Wednesday afternoon being led down to the station and learnt that between eight and twelve of them are consigned to a Cambridge horse slaughterer every fortnight. Since one hardly ever sees a horse either in the field or in the streets these days, one can't help wondering whether they all come from to provide such a steady traffic.

I asked Mr Richards if the branch would be kept open or whether there were any plans for its closure, and it seems that no one has suggested closing it yet, although it is constantly kept under review by the railway administration along with other lines.

I also asked if it were likely to be dieselised, but this was something which nobody had any information to give. I wondered whether steam railcars would be the answer to these branch lines, but I was told that these were now obsolete, and had been replaced by diesels. But steam or diesel, the Llanfyllin branch is still very much alive and everyone hopes that it will remain so.

A rare photo taken from between the church and the river, on the bridge that carried the A483 over the Llanfyllin line. The photographer was in England, the train in Wales
(Jack Beeston)

ABOVE *On September 2, 1961, 46511 comes off the Llanfyllin line, going towards Llanymynech (Gerald T Robinson)*

BELOW *Ivatt 45311 arrives at Llansanffraid (known as Llansaintffraid by the Cambrian and Llansantffraid by the GWR) as it heads towards Llanymynech*

ABOVE *At Llanfyllin station, 46519 is about to leave for Llanymynech and Oswestry with an up passenger, while on the right 46401 waits with its goods train*

BELOW *Also at Llanfyllin is Ivatt 2MT 46515*

ABOVE *On June 4, 1954, 'Dukedog' 4-4-0 No 9017 leaves Llanymynech with an Aberystwyth to Whitchurch train*

BELOW *In 1962, 46512 passes through Llanymynech with an Up goods*
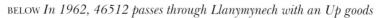

ABOVE *6371 with the 12.25 Welshpool to Whitchurch train (B Morrison)*

BELOW *May 16, 1956, 'Dukedog' 4-4-0 No 9008 departs*

ABOVE *Ivatt 2 MT Class 2-6-0 No 46520 approaches Llanymynech with the 8.15 from Four Crosses workers train, all stations to Oswestry, September 2, 1961 (Gerald T Robinson)*

BELOW *Apparently a very windy day, and there's a huge amount of smoke coming from Ivatt 2 MT Class 2-6-0 as it pulls into Llanymynech – so smoky it's not possible to see if it's a passenger or goods train. The yard, though, is deserted of wagons, which is a sign the line is near closure – the yard closed on July 6, 1964 (Neil Parkhouse collection)*

ABOVE *Llanymynech in April 1960, and Ivatt 46527 pulls away with a Llanfyllin to Oswestry train*

BELOW *7800 Torquay Manor arrives at Llanymynech with the 08.20 Oswestry to Aberystwyth train on September 2, 1961 (Gerald T Robinson)*

ABOVE *October 24, 1964, 46510 departs with the 13.30 Llanfyllin to Oswestry*

LEFT *A tablet for the single line between Llansanffraid and Llanymynech, to be passed to the driver to allow the engine to proceed*

RIGHT *A later token for Pool Quay to Llanymynech*

BELOW *80096 arrives with the Oswestry to Welshpool local, the Shropshire & Montgomeryshire track having been removed and the Evalast block factory in the process of being built*

ABOVE *Just after nationalisation, June 15, 1948, and the track to the S&MR is double tracked*

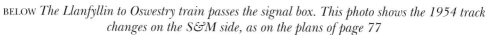

BELOW *The Llanfyllin to Oswestry train passes the signal box. This photo shows the 1954 track changes on the S&M side, as on the plans of page 77*

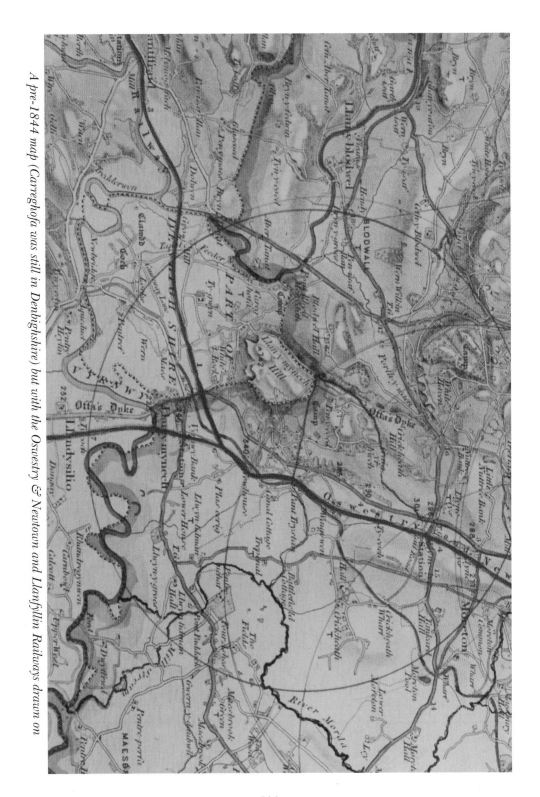

A pre-1844 map (Carreghofa was still in Denbighshire) but with the Oswestry & Newtown and Llanfyllin Railways drawn on

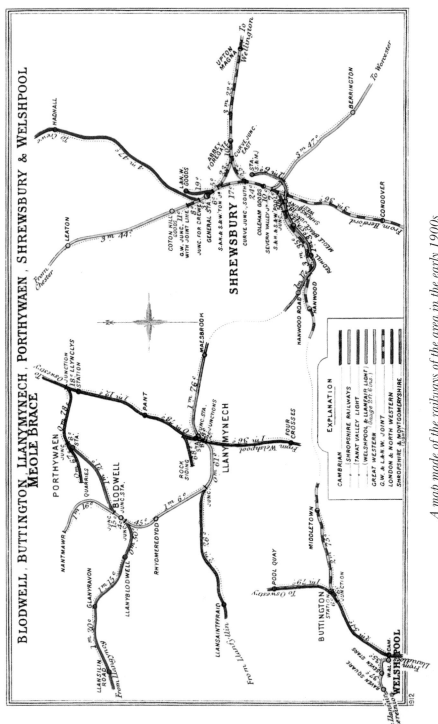

A map made of the railways of the area in the early 1900s

ABOVE *46523 arriving at Llanymynech*

BELOW *BR Standard Class 4 4-6-0 No 75029, leaking steam as it leaves Llanymynech with the Welshpool to Oswestry train (the iron mink truck in the sidings – see page 124)*

At the end of the war the ammunition depots around Nesscliff and Kinnerley were kept open for another fourteen years. Once the decision to close them was made, the railway was offered to the British Transport Commission, the railways having by then been nationalised. The BTC decided to close the railway, and the last stone trains from Criggion ran in December 1959.

No 189 with the SLS Rail tour of May 22, 1955 (Brian Hilton)

ABOVE *On June 11, 1959, the S&M yard, looking towards Maesbrook. The shed on the right had been a timber merchants and Barraclough's clog factory (K Bannister)*

BELOW *The original Potts station building at Llanymynech, looking in good condition after almost 100 years (K Bannister)*

ABOVE *The name board on the Cambrian Railways side, the S&M building behind*
BELOW *A leaflet announcing the new halt at Carreghofa, and one for an excursion for ramblers from Liverpool to the Llanymynech area*

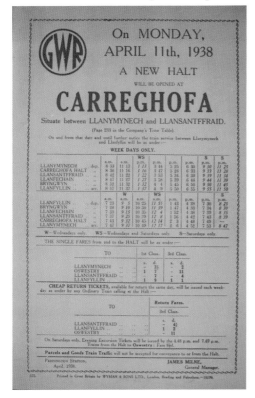
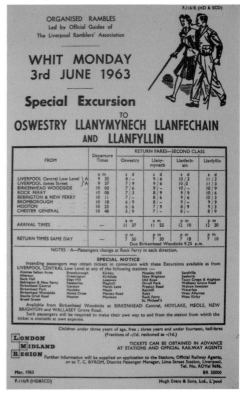

On 29 February 1960 the Shropshire & Montgomeryshire Light Railway was closed, though the last train was a Stephenson Locomotive Society excursion on 20 March. This was the report of that excursion, in the Advertizer of March 23, 1960, with the heading:

Passengers had black-edged tickets
for farewell run on an old railway line

Many people turned out on Sunday afternoon to pay their farewell tribute to a line that has served the district for nearly a century – the old Shropshire and Montgomeryshire Light Railway. To mark the occasion the Stephenson Locomotive Society ran a special – the last train – from Hookagate to Llanymynech. Its passengers were 140 members of the society and at Llanymynech crowds of local people lined the track as the train drew up. The crew of the engine were Mr Harold Lloyd of Pant, driver, and Mr George Beeston, Llanymynech, firemen. It was the third time the line had been officially closed. The first was in 1866. It was reopened in 1868 but closed again twelve years later. It was finally reopened again in 1911. In spite of extensive rebuilding by the War Office, the line still retains its character to a surprising degree and on the Criggion line it presents much the same picture as it did in the 1880s. And now, after a life of almost a century, the line has finally closed.

*Three photos of the last train along the Shropshire & Montgomeryshire Light Railway, March
20, 1960, with many Llanymynech characters
(*OPPOSITE *K Bannister,* TOP *Graham Vincent)*

Two photos of Llanymynech station in 2012
ABOVE *The entrance (compare with page 80)*
BELOW *The Cambrian Railways weighbridge office and GWR iron mink truck. The truck used to be on the bay platform as a safe storage hut for lamps and fuel, being metal*

ABOVE *The site of Carreghofa Halt, in 2012, looking towards Llanfyllin and Nantmawr*

BELOW *The road bridge at Llanymynech, now with metal supports but also a weight limit. This is taken from the track bed, looking towards Four Crosses, in 2012*

ABOVE *Around 1963, 0-6-0 Collett goods No 2251 enters Llanymynech with the Down passenger to Welshpool*

BELOW *A similar time, 46513 with the Oswestry to Llanfyllin train*

ABOVE *7828 Odney Manor*

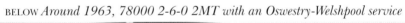

BELOW *Around 1963, 78000 2-6-0 2MT with an Oswestry-Welshpool service*

ABOVE *The site of Pant Station in 2012, with very close to the same view as on page 95, the white van here where the station house was*
BELOW *The skew bridge at Well House Lane, Pant, in 2012. This shows what an impressively large – and expensive – structure and embankment it was*

ABOVE *7812 Erlestoke Manor on the up platform. Behind, on the left, the Evalast factory that made concrete blocks, later Boral Edenhall (Russell Mulford)*

BELOW *46509 on the same platform*

ABOVE *An ex-Cambrian engine with a goods from Welshpool*
BELOW *A diesel multiple unit on an Aberystwyth-Shrewsbury service, diverted through Llanymynech, passes the signal box. It was said that the Welshpool to Oswestry line 'died with dignity', in that it never had a DMU on its tracks. Though some might wish it had rather kept open and lost its dignity, this rather faded photo is proof it didn't even do that (Jack Beeston)*

Dr Beeching and his razor gang
THE THREAT OF CLOSURE

Straight after nationalisation in 1948 there had been a threat to the Llanfyllin line, and talk of closure grew. Even before the Beeching plan of 1963 the Mid Wales line from Llanidloes to Brecon was closed. Now came the report that was to destroy the railways around Llanymynech.

These were some of the reactions from the local councils reported by the Advertizer on April 9, 1963:

Councils' joint decision on Beeching plans

A joint meeting of Oswestry Borough and Rural Councils decided on Wednesday to recommend to the government that a commission should be set up with a view to greater cooperation between all types of transport. And that until such a commission is set up the Beeching plan for the railways of Britain should be shelved.

"The livelihood of Oswestry," the Mayor of Oswestry, Councillor GA Davis, said, "is dependent on the railway." He said that there were literally thousands of people coming to the town by rail, because they liked Oswestry for their shopping. "This report is premature," he added, "the government should look into the whole transport system of the country." The mayor added that if 70,000 people were sacked by British Railways, they would all have to be paid dole money. "The roads of this country are in no state to meet the requirements of the present time. Already there is one vehicle for every 30 yards of road. Can you imagine what it will be like with additional traffic if the railways are closed? We must tell Dr Beeching [*then the chairman of BR*] and his razor gang that we are in no position to accept the proposals. We must not take this lying down."

Councillor RD Jones told the meeting, "Dr Beeching was given five years to make the railways pay. First reports said that a third of the country's railways would be closed. Now that figure has leapt to two thirds. I believe that Mr Marples [*the Minister of Transport*] is very biased against the railways. If transport as a whole is looked at through a magnifying glass, it would be a much better thing. Road haulage is nothing but a rat race, and I make no apology to anyone for saying that. There are 400,000 goods vehicles on roads today that are not fit."

"I've a feeling that I'm the odd man out," commented Councillor E Bowen. "I agree with Dr Beeching. I think that he has done a first-class job. It is the people of this country who are closing the railways. They are using practically any other form of transport rather than use the railways. We must be realistic and see things as they are today. We have heard a lot of railwaymen at this meeting, I must sympathise with them if they lose their jobs. But other jobs will come along. As far as I can see the Oswestry-

Welshpool line could never be made to pay."

Councillor J Strange commented, "Any fool can cut off the parts that don't pay. The difficulty is in making those parts pay. There are some lines that should be kept open on the national expense as a social service."

Councillor RD Jones proposed that the recommendations of the Beeching report should be shelved until the commission could look into the whole question of transport. The resolution was passed unanimously.

Of course, their resolution was ignored by the government, and in December Beeching announced the closure of the Whitchurch to Welshpool line. Oswestry's new mayor attempted to save the line.

Oswestry's Mayor goes into battle to save line

A lead to the public in a fight to save the railway passenger service between Whitchurch and Welshpool via Oswestry, is given this week by the Mayor, Councillor DJ Howells, a ticket collector at Oswestry station. News that Dr Beeching had raised his axe before bringing it down on the local service came earlier this week – an unwelcome prelude to the Christmas holiday. Although himself a railwayman, Councillor Howells is due to retire in March. He enters the battle, therefore in the interests of the town and of his fellow workers.

"Do nothing and you've lost your rail service forever. Personally, this is a sad blow to the town of Oswestry, which has always been known as a railway town. It is obvious that the wage packets from the railway industry will be much less, with, no doubt, serious effect on the trade in and around Oswestry. I do appeal to the traders and the general public to do all that they possibly can to retain our rail service. Watch your local paper and railway premises for the announcement of the date of the proposals, and post your objections at the appropriate time."

From the Advertizer, December 25, 1963

If there were any objections they were ignored, as they were throughout the country. In fact Beeching had given a better passenger rating to the line from Whitchurch to Welshpool (5000 to 10,000 passengers a week) than Shrewsbury to Welshpool. Even so, two years later it was decided to close the line from Whitchurch to Welshpool, via Oswestry and Llanymynech. The Llanfyllin line would close at the same time.

This was part of the editorial in the Advertizer on January 20, 1965, and only the second topic of the column, to show its lack of importance:

It will seem strange this week without passenger trains on the Welshpool-Oswestry-Whitchurch and the Llanfyllin-Llanymynech lines, but from the purely economic point of view it was hard to make a case for their retention when one knows full well that frequently trains ran on them with a mere handful of passengers. Yet as link by link goes by the cutting out of these branch lines it surely must follow that with the loss of the many little feeders there must be fewer passengers for the mainlines. And as a service to the community the lines were valuable, but no one was willing to face up to those implications.

There was also a comment in the reporting of the last train from Whitchurch to Welshpool on Saturday afternoon that seemed to question whether Llanymynech really wanted its railway:

> Most noticeable feature of the outward trip was the interest shown at all the stations between Whitchurch and Oswestry, and the almost complete lack of it on the stations between Oswestry and Welshpool. Why this should be I can't explain, but it was apparent that there was an element in the population lying between the first two towns which regarded their rail link with some affection, which came to the surface and manifested itself on the line's last day.

This was the report of the last train, from Suzanne Hughes, as she recorded the final scene at Oswestry after previously travelling from Llanfyllin:

> It was a dark and stormy night when the driver said to the fireman, "Sound the whistle"… and with a defiant scream the last train steamed out Oswestry Station at 9.25 on Sunday night. While the driving sleet hissed and spattered, the rearing furnace, tended by fireman Dennis Butler, of Ellesmere, flickered and glowed, lighting up the small band of people that stood huddled round the engine, No 7832, Foxcote Manor – to wave goodbye. With about twenty passengers on board, veteran Driver Jack Holloway, of Llanymynech [*Jack Holloway lived along the Wern at Llanymynech, near Carreghofa Halt; he died not long after closure*], and Guard Arthur Meredith of Oswestry, took their last journey on the doomed line to Whitchurch.

These two pages: the last two days at Llanymynech (all Russell Mulford)
ABOVE *The SLS special from Llanfyllin, 46512 pulling five coaches, passes the signal box on January 17, 1965*
BELOW *The last scheduled train, 75026 BR standard 4-6-0 4MT, on January 16, 1965*

ABOVE *75026 moves away from Llanymynech*

BELOW *Porter Dennis Evans, known as Spindle, doesn't look as distressed as perhaps he should, as he talks to Hector & Nellie Beeston (Hector was a former signalman from Llanymynech, Nellie ran the refreshments rooms), and 75026 disappears round the bend*

The end of the line
CLOSURE & DEMOLITION

Just over 100 years after the Oswestry & Newtown Railway was built with such a tremendous struggle, the line was casually and almost carelessly closed. The Llanymynech to Buttington line closed for goods September 7, 1964, and for passengers January 18, 1965. The Llanymynech to Llanfyllin line closed for goods November 2, 1964, and for passengers January 18, 1965. Llynclys junction to Llanymynech closed for goods November 2, 1964, and for passengers on January 18, 1965. The only line in the area that remained open was that from Gobowen to Nantmawr quarries, and later Llanddu quarry, for a weekly freight working. At least a few yards of this was the old Potts branch to Nantmawr. The last freight working ran, according to Mike Lloyd, on October 28, 1988, with official closure on October 3, 1993.

When the other lines were closed in 1965 they were quickly destroyed. The track was taken up, bridges – including the one over the Vyrnwy replaced only eight years previously – removed, and the track way and station area sold or rented out by British Railways. The Cambrian side of Llanymynech station became a coal depot. The Potts area and yard was used by Evalast and then Boral Edenhall to make concrete blocks. Their works were demolished, and in 2008 a housing estate built, Badgers Green, with a road called Heritage Way (the opportunity to call it the Old Potts Road was spurned, though S&M Street, after the Shropshire and Montgomeryshire, might have been misunderstood).

Pant Station after closure, the name boards having been removed

The Vyrnwy bridge, replaced just nine years before, being demolished. Removal of the line started at Buttington, and moved north to Oswestry (Jack Beeston)

The track bed at the site of Carreghofa Halt is used for cattle, though there is a new house just above called Carreghofa Halt. The cutting around Wern junction, where the Llanfyllin spur left the Nantmawr branch, was used as a landfill site during the 1980s. Pant station buildings were demolished, as was the house, despite the occupants asking if they could buy it.

The Cambrian Railways side of Llanymynech station is an empty area, now for sale. In the 1980s, when the Llanymynech and Pant bypass got as close as it's ever done to being made, the plan was to use the old track bed between the crossing over the Vyrnwy and Llynclys. Later plans, though, moved the bypass further east, avoiding the railway. This meant that the road would have crossed the railway track bed near Llynclys, at Ty Coch farm. As there was no track there the road would have eliminated any possibility of the railway ever being used, so the Cambrian Railways Society quickly put down half a mile of track on the section between Llynclys and Penygarreg Lane, Pant. The bypass plans came as usual to nothing, but there is still the track, used by the Cambrian Heritage Railways (successor to the Cambrian Railways Society) to store rolling stock and run short trips. There are hopes to connect with the line from Gobowen to Llynclys Junction, a section that was mothballed after the last quarry train in 1988.

But it is extremely doubtful that the track could ever return to Llanymynech itself. There are too many obstacles at Pant – not the problems that the original contractors of the Oswestry and Newtown Railway had, tramways and the canal to go over and difficult cuttings through the hard rock, but because sections of the track bed were sold to private owners and are in use.

ABOVE *Llanymynech signal box being dismantled (Barrie Kelsall)*

BELOW *Dismantling of the station under way in July, 1966 (Barrie Kelsall)*

ABOVE *Another view of the demolition of Llanymynech signal box in July, 1966, as England (and Bobby Charlton) win the World Cup (Barrie Kelsall)*

BELOW *Llanymynech yard after closure*

The waste

LAST THOUGHTS

Looking back it's easy to curse the governments of the 1960s for their closing of so many railways, and in this case those that served Llanymynech.
But those were the days when the old was going to be swept away, and what was
going to replace it was what Harold Wilson, Prime Minister in the second half
of the 1960s, called 'the white heat of the technological revolution' – motor-
ways and lorries and cars – fast and adaptable, instead of slow and polluting
steam locomotives on fixed and inconvenient tracks. Buses could serve towns
and villages much more cheaply and flexibly than the railways. Many of the
towns and villages of the old Cambrian Railways area had seen their popula-
tions go down in the fifty years after the First World War. Railways were hugely
inefficient, with steam trains using up coal, needing a driver and a fireman
and a guard for a couple of passengers.

On the other hand, it isn't just using hindsight to suggest that closing a
functioning means of transport is a mistake: in the edition of the Advertizer
that announced the railway closures was an article deploring "Road chaos", so
in 1963, at the same time as people were asking what could be done to cure
traffic problems the connection didn't seemed to be made that encouraging
people to buy cars would not help. And of course there wasn't the awareness
of the corruption in high places: that Ernest Marples, the Minister for Transport, was the director of and had connections with several road building firms,
and railways were considered an obstacle to making money by building roads.
But we've always had a different attitude to roads. They are a utility we take
completely for granted. Imagine a Beeching report on the roads: "Withdrawal
of road services. The B4398 will be discontinued as from Monday, due to loss-
making. The road will be dug up. Tenders for the land are invited."

What we can genuinely regret is the finality of the closures, the arrogant
certainty that something that had taken years to build and such energy and
money to keep, was finished with forever. In 1880 the Potts line from Shrewsbury to Llanymynech was closed, but the track remained, so that when Colonel Stephens reopened it he could simply replace the sleepers and repair the
way. It was different in 1965. Almost immediately stations and bridges were
demolished, the track lifted, and much of the line sold to private owners. The
bridge at Llanymynech over the Vyrnwy had been replaced in 1957. It was
removed on closure when at the very least it could have been left for walkers
or cyclists, as could the whole line.

In other countries uneconomic railways are closed but mothballed. Not
here. Many of the towns and villages between Oswestry and Welshpool are
growing, especially Llanymynech, Pant, and Arddleen. People now use trains
more. There is a preference for trains over buses, especially as trains connect

with other routes. The UK now has its highest passenger figures for trains since the 1920s. Had the track, or at least the track bed, been preserved, it is easy to imagine a single line between Gobowen and Welshpool through Llanymynech, with diesel multiple units connecting to the main lines to Chester, Birmingham, and elsewhere. This isn't nostalgia, it's a realistic solution to our transport problems. I firmly believe that if by some chance the line had been left open in the 1960s, Llanymynech Railway Station would now be a busy place, with a large car park, rivalling the success of Gobowen station. Instead, with the track and bridges gone, parcels of land sold, buildings and a coal yard on the old track bed, Llanymynech station is a deserted and empty plot. The village doesn't even have a bypass to take away those replacements of the railways that were meant to make everything wonderful, the cars and lorries that pollute and clog up the roads.

The demolition train with BR Standard Class 4 No 75010 reaches Llanymynech in 1966.
The ground frame for the yard has already been removed, on the right. The road bridge,
in the background, that carries the B4398 over the old track bed, is still owned by BRB (a
subsidiary of Network Rail). It seems that whenever road and rail crossed, the responsibility for
maintaining the level crossing or bridge was always the railway's, even now, almost 50 years
after closure – which is one reason the railways never paid: they were never allowed to
(John Humphreys)

141

Index

B
Beeching 131, 132, 140
Blodwel junction 40, 70
British Railways 3, 88, 99, 131, 136
Brunel 5, 8, 29
Buttington 16, 17, 31, 89, 103, 136, 137
C
Cambrian Railways 3, 6, 24, 25, 26, 27, 34, 40, 47, 48, 59, 64, 65, 67, 70, 72, 78, 81, 99, 121, 124, 137, 140, 142, 143
Carreghofa Halt 3, 28, 29, 30, 31, 39, 40, 43, 73, 104, 105, 116, 121, 125, 133, 137
Bobby Charlton 87, 139
Homersham Cox 38
Crickheath tramway 18
D
David Davies 17, 66
E
Ellesmere Canal 7
F
Four Crosses 3, 4, 46, 52, 78, 90, 91, 92, 93, 104, 112, 125
FE Fox-Davies 27, 32, 34, 39, 41, 53, 54, 56, 59
RS France 29, 32, 34
G
Gazelle 56, 63, 87
Great Western Railway 3, 5, 6, 8, 11, 25, 29, 32, 46, 51, 65, 66, 67, 68, 70, 71, 73, 87, 99, 108, 124
H
Jack Holloway 91, 133
Dolly Hopton 47, 51
John Edward Humphreys 85, 87, 88, 89, 92, 94
William Henry Humphreys 89, 96
J
Llewelyn Jones 3, 102, 103
Tom Jones 47, 50, 51

L
Lake Vyrnwy 52
Llandysilio 16, 19, 51
Llangynog 28, 29, 30, 31, 40, 53, 68, 99
Llanidloes 8, 9, 13, 17, 19, 24, 66, 88, 131
Llansanffraid 16, 21, 22, 106, 107, 108
Llanyblodwel 26, 30, 31, 32, 34, 40
Llanymynech signal box 3, 27, 45, 138, 139
Llynclys 18, 20, 40, 47, 52, 53, 89, 99, 136, 137, 144
London & North Western Railway 5, 8, 29, 32, 99
M
Manchester 5, 6, 8, 13, 16, 24, 25, 33, 44, 50, 62, 85, 87, 106
Meifod 16, 30, 43
Milford Haven 5, 6, 8, 13, 24
Montgomeryshire Canal 7, 143
N
Nantmawr 3, 29, 31, 34, 39, 40, 42, 53, 64, 73, 99, 125, 136, 137
Nantmawr Junction 39, 42
North Wales Wagon Company 85
O
Oswestry & Border Counties Advertiser/Advertizer 4, 8, 9, 10, 11, 13, 16, 19, 20, 21, 22, 23, 24, 29, 31, 33, 35, 36, 38, 43, 48, 50, 52, 57, 60, 62, 65, 68, 102, 103, 106, 122, 131, 132, 140, 144
Oswestry and Newtown Railway 5, 9, 13, 15, 17, 18, 19, 20, 21, 29, 94, 137
George Owen 17, 40, 66
P
Pant Station 2, 3, 12, 95, 128, 136
Porthywaen 18, 29
Potteries, Shrewsbury and North Wales Railway 3, 32
Potts Railway 18, 28, 30, 32, 55, 56

Prince of Wales 10, 52, 67
R
Richard Reeves 34, 53
River Vyrnwy 7, 13, 15, 102
Richard Roberts 73
Rock Siding 26, 40, 42, 86
S
Thomas Savin 17, 21, 22, 32, 66
Shrewsbury and North Wales Railway 3, 5, 6, 29, 30, 31, 32, 33
Shrewsbury and Welshpool Railway 9, 17

Shropshire & Montgomeryshire 3, 56, 62, 64, 114, 122, 123, 143
Stephens 53, 56, 57, 58, 59, 61, 64, 140
T
Tanat Valley Light Railway 40, 53, 143
Tanat Valley Railway 53
James Thompson 38
V
Vyrnwy 7, 13, 15, 16, 23, 52, 77, 102, 104, 136, 137, 140
W
West Shropshire Mineral Railway 3, 21, 29

Sources

Great Western Journal no 61, the Llanfyllin Branch	John Copsey & Chris Turner
The Cambrian Railways	RW Kidner
The Cambrian Railways	Rex Christiansen & RW Miller
Cambrian Lines	Rex Christiansen
The Story of the Cambrian	CP Gasquoine
Cambrian Railways Album	CC Green
Shropshire & Montgomeryshire Light Railway	Peter Johnson
Shropshire & Montgomeryshire Light Railway	Keith & Susan Turner
S&M Light Railway under military control	Mike Christensen
The Criggion Branch of the S&M Light Railway	Roger Carpenter
The Llanfyllin Railway	Lewis Cozens
The Shropshire & Montgomeryshire Railway	Eric S Tonks
The Tanat Valley Light Railway	Mike Lloyd
Branch line to Shrewsbury	Vic Mitchell & Keith Smith
Branch Lines round Oswestry	Vic Mitchell & Keith Smith
Lost Railways of Shropshire	Leslie Oppitz
Montgomeryshire Canal	John Horsley Denton
Documents concerning the parish of Llanymynech	Shropshire Parish Collections
Montgomeryshire Records	Montgomeryshire Genealogical Society

For more on Llanymynech, see the 'On the border' website
http://www.llanymynechandpant.co.uk

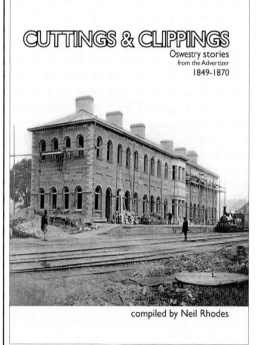